THE MYTH OF GENDER

WRITTEN & ILLUSTRATED

BY

S. G. MUNE

COUR·AGE

IS TO TELL THE STORY OF
WHO YOU ARE
WITH YOUR WHOLE HEART.

-DR. BRENE BROWN

BY PURCHASING THIS BOOK...

**You help one teacher
reach more students through the internet
one conversation at a time.**

For Blue.
Who taught me gender is blind,
But the love of comedy will always see us through

And for my Mother,
For the years you sacrificed yourself
so that someday I could be Me;
I'm grateful.

JOIN THE CONVERSATION &

DONATE   TODAY

www.facebook.com/MythofGender

THANK YOU FOR YOUR SUPPORT

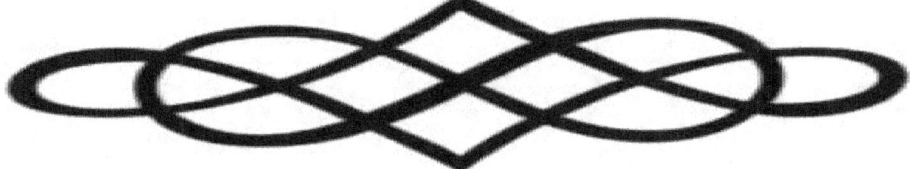

Published by Gender Atheist Publication

CONTENTS

INTRO TO IDENTITY

LANGUAGE IS POWER

MY BODY

GENDER & ORIENTATION

THE ART OF OBJECTION

PORTRAIT OF A QWEIRDO

SCRATCH PAPER

INTRO TO IDENTITY

My mama's weather worn farmhouse was the world's last line of defense against her six wild eyed country kids.

I remember a miniature version of me tapping on her leg, crying, "Mama! What's *wrong* with me? Why am I so different?"

I pleaded for her to explain the world to me.

I was the only left-handed, curly haired, freckled version of the bunch.

My mama pinched her eyebrows together and gave me an answer I wasn't prepared for:

"I don't know." She frowned.

That's when it dawned on me.

I must have a real bad case of this being different.

ONE YEAR LATER...

I watched Fozzie Bear, Kermit, and Gonzo unload from a cargo plane in *The Muppets take Manhattan*. Stamped on their shipping crates read: "Bear", "Frog", "*Whatever*".

"Oh! *A Whatever!* That's what *I* am!" I was delighted to find inclusion in my own definition.

Gonzo the Great then became the first TV icon I could identify with for many years to come.

FASTFOWARD>> 4TH GRADE

The jungle gym was famous for our daily standoffs between Good versus Evil.

The boys wanted to rescue the girls from our jungle gym prison.

It was the girl's job to cry for help until they were rescued.

I hated this job.

So instead, I became the Squid Monster.

It was my job to guard against any attempt of girl rescue while taking anyone hostage within my strong squid-like grasp.

We were stumped when, in a moment of oversight, we all ended up in prison *together*.

The Girls. The Boys. And the most powerful Squid Monster in the universe.

I spent my early teens and 20's defining what it was my mother couldn't put into words. I was determined to follow my own compass. Loving my differently-gendered identity gave me more power, vigor, and wildness than anything I had ever known. The concept of being transgender didn't actually occur to me until I was nearly 24, but by that time I'd been living as a gender atheist for about 8 years. Converging this with my identity as an Agobi healer was a *natural* part of my evolution towards *wholeness*.

I now see what a precious gift my unique blend of perspectives bring to those around me. As an Agobi, I help others explore *their* identity by validating their "I" and granting them fresh language to continue to create that identity for others to understand.

Language [i.e. communication] is the only way we can exist to each other. With every new aspect of identity, you may find yourself profoundly *changed*; And this is a book of power identities, indeed! My commitment to you is to be clear and clearly known by you so that you may delight yourself with the possibilities you find within your *own* gender and identity!

Here in your hand is the *first ever* heirloom of key insights into the human identity from the perspective of a traveling Transgender Agobi. Now that I'm older, it is important for me to take on my role as a bearded *Abuela* (grandmother). It's my turn to retell my gendered adventures to encourage, comfort, and direct you on your path to a *loved identity*.

A *loved* identity makes *anything* possible. It unearths your greatness as you begin to own these 5 principles of Identity:

1. *There is no such thing as inauthentic identity.*
Gender identity isn't *real*. We created it.
Therefore, it cannot be fake *either*.

2. The purpose of creating you is *solely* to enjoy what you've created. Period.
Anything more is either bonus material or false advertising.

3. We must suspend our need to police and moralize others so we can extend that same privilege to *ourselves*.

4. We protect ourselves from self-hatred by *being* the consummate lover of our own *persona*.

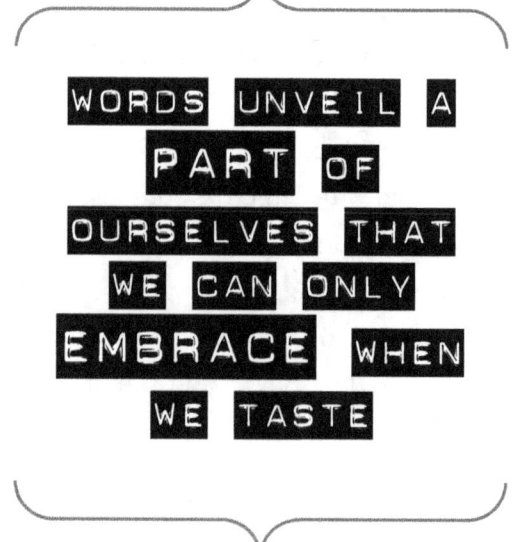

WORDS UNVEIL A PART OF OURSELVES THAT WE CAN ONLY EMBRACE WHEN WE TASTE

5. We are *destined* to shatter perceptions *only* when we *gladly* exist.
   We exist through our conversations.

The world taught me that being a gender atheist was heresy, but I refused to listen. Instead of self-destructing, I slathered my life with generous portions of *self care* and emotional *bravado,* relentlessly storming obstacles with passion and purpose.

As an Agobi, I am destined to *only* appear to people at the crossroads of their identity, so be aware!

As this new path opens up for you, other things in your life will also come to a *close*.

I've seen entire lives turned over at the foot of this path, so take courage!

As you discover new forms of Identity, may this book of short stories ever be your guide to finding your Self again, *with your own words.*

WHETHER YOU SUCCEED
OR NOT
IS IRRELEVENT, THERE
IS NO SUCH THING.
MAKING
THE UNKNOWN
KNOWN IS WHAT IS
IMPORTANT.

-GEORGIA O'KEEFFE

I relish this notion that "I" might exist beyond the confines of *language*; beyond society's "common sense". For example, this insipid need to know my ethnicity by 'checking the box' on surveys.

 This first inspired me to evolve my identity as an environmental defense, colorful and conspicuous as a jester's hat. So when I'm asked what my ethnic (color) is, I answer them with the same insane logic with which they asked. I write:

"OFF-WHITE"

 Unless I'm feeling peckish, in which case, I note: "*-usually. But green today*".

As a general rule, I keep my identity springy and optimistic through sardonic *social adaptation*. I do this by generating equally irrelevant yet far more enjoyable answers to the irritating questions being asked.

If you're someone like me who feels their energy drain from them whenever answering questions like "What is your identity?" *why not* answer with the same line of nonsense from which the question is being asked? Who can say that *we* don't know _____ about ourselves? Or who can say what we said about ourselves is *wrong*?

Nonsense!

Hijack their questionnaires they make to inform them about you. If they can't neatly fit you or your identity into a box, they might as well *enjoy* a lively response in the box marked *Other*!

I sidestep this mad narration of my gender identity with enthusiasm and mischievousness. I only drop in on surveys to see if anyone's still listening. On more than a few occasions, especially in institutes of power, I hear it echo up the halls as I walk away: *Laughter*.

Isn't that the point of identity? *To feel alive?*

By spreading this hysterically mad gender myth, I'm no longer a slave to all the boxes being hurled at me. The things they worry about are *not* my concern. They'll continue to make more boxes for *only* those identities they want to acknowledge. That's their job.

Yours is to speak your truth.

You don't need these boxes in order to exist. You exist whenever you speak your truth.

There's a whole new world of identity outside these boxes just waiting for us to play with it.

So next time you get a survey asking you to define your Self, by all means give them an earful!

It's not important whether they have a box ready to hold you in *yet*.

DARE TO BELIEVE THAT THE RISK OF LIVING IS LIFE ITSELF, AND THOSE WHO NEVER DARE, NEVER LIVE.

-S.G.MUNE, 16

THINGS YOU WILL NEED:
~~HAMMER~~
~~LOGIC~~
~~BFS~~
HUMOR
AND A GOOD PAIR OF ASS KICKIN' BOOTS

When you identify with *something* and later decide it isn't who you are anymore, it's natural for the people around you to struggle with your initial transition. This is called Identity Shift Resistance. There is this myth that adult identities are concrete. However, healthy identities *continually* shift throughout our lives as we take on new interests and experiences.

Let me give you an example from my life: I once experimented to understand who how "I", my identity, showed up in the world. So for an entire year, I talked endlessly about my love of giraffes. In actuality, I could've cared less about these lanky land creatures, but for that year I was determined to spread my "giraffe" loving identity *everywhere*. I pointed out giraffes, talked about giraffes, looked for giraffes, learned what I could about giraffes, and spoke of it whenever I could with polite company. I adopted the word "Giraffe" as an artificial part of my identity. In this way, I would be sure to know when people echoed my 'identity' back to me.

Was the world listening?

The result? Despite my actual mental boredom on the subject, I received meaningful articles, stuffed animals, greeting cards, trinkets, many conversations, and a number of unsolicited invitations on the subject of giraffes from other people. I took this magical moment as an invitation:

The world wanted to play with me, I just had to say *how*.

At the end of the year, I had grown quite a collection of giraffes, all manifestations of this delicious secret I had quite clearly plagued my language with. It had now become a part of my identity to others. If anyone asked, I was the 'giraffe guy'.

Furthermore, I had made giraffes *literally* appear in my office and my life *without* any use of my own talent, time, or money. When the year was over, I decided to reverse the seed I had sewn and entirely *erased* the word "giraffe" from my vocabulary.

This is when I became acutely aware of identity shift resistance.

I didn't respond to 'giraffe' in conversation. I hid my trinkets. I politely turned down invitations. I thanked people for giraffe memorabilia, but would avoid mulling it over in conversation. Within two weeks, people around the water cooler were clearly concerned about the relationship between me and my giraffes. I was surprised that people became acutely aware of my oral divorce to the word *giraffe*. Within the month, they focused all their worry on me, mistaking my sudden disinterest with depression or illness. At this point it became clear that if I didn't do something to fill the void, this would turn into a giraffe-tastrophy.

I decided to give out many invitations to my *most* social friends to do *other* things with me that were unrelated to giraffes, but that I *actually* enjoyed. And after I let them see me happy and well, my most social friends quickly spread the word to call off my impending intervention.

After two months, my friends finally got over the absence of my long-neck compadre and stopped mentioning it themselves. After three months, I had successfully moved my entire herd of friends over to more personally gratifying parts of my identity and donated the rest of my giraffes to the goodwill three towns over.

During this time I realized that who "*I am*" in conversation is a powerful invitation for others to participate in my life. As I describe myself, I align with an image ("place artificial stereotype here") that others will make into *my* assumed 'role', *even against my will.*

In this same way, if you're the 'funny guy' you may find it difficult to have a normal 'bad day'.

If you're the 'girl who studies a lot', you may find you weren't given an invitation simply because people assumed you would be studying, even if you were free that particular night.

Understand, you don't avoid a "giraffe" identity by telling people you *don't* like giraffes. Or you don't like being fat. Or you aren't a (boy/girl).

It only causes the "giraffe" they are envisioning to *linger.*

You have to create a life absent of your past 'giraffe' and fill it with something else.

If you want to change from being seen as 'the study girl', don't let people see you with books out, or invite friends over twice a month for pizza and movies *without discussing school.*

Show up as the *kind* of friend you want to be seen as. Conversations must be replaced with new ones. Realize that, no matter what "image" you align with, it only exists because *you keep talking/dwelling on it.*

If you don't like what role you play, simply refuse it's association and replace it with something more enthusiastic. After that, allow time with your new language to weave a pleasant new "you"; and one you do enjoy so much *more.*

Seriously. Be patient with your friends and family and it's that delightfully, disgustingly simple.

It simply takes replacing that undesirable thing you *allow* in conversation.

Don't believe it's that simple?

Pick an animal of topic for one year. It'll give you a fresh perspective on how your identity shows up in conversation, and *who* is really listening.

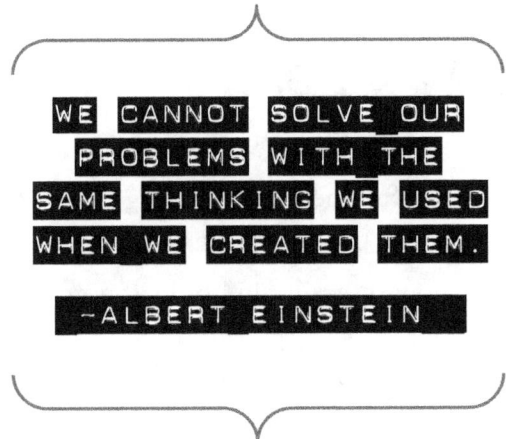

WE CANNOT SOLVE OUR PROBLEMS WITH THE SAME THINKING WE USED WHEN WE CREATED THEM.

-ALBERT EINSTEIN

"Each step towards your true identity is an essential task to attaining total enlightenment."

Now realize this statement is *full of shit.*
And, if you didn't hear the baloney the first time, go back and reread it. The first lesson I learned in attaining enlightenment is:

IF IT AIN'T LIGHT, IT AIN'T ENLIGHTENMENT

To be enlightened is to "breathe easy". Life is a staircase that goes nowhere. Progress is an illusion. Life is cyclical; it is a dance around the floor. Keep in mind that other's opinion on what is actually occurring *to you* is about as accurate as a blind man's painting of Picasso; without the use of a canvas. The *point* of Self-help books is to define a problem that *wasn't there before*. Self-help seekers are some of the most problem-riddled people I know. Authors of self-help books simply re-arrange concepts to create a *new* sense of false journeying from a *have-not* to a hopeful sense of *trying* to have.
This strikes me as a subliminal child's message: An endless game of 'catch some worthiness'.
At first this sense of journeying can be helpful, but this paradigm is doomed to fail because it is the pursuit to end the sacred hunger. Nature shows us that we are never finished, and nothing travels that does not tend to return. Satisfaction is *meant* to be fleeting; otherwise fullness would be a once-in-a-lifetime event.

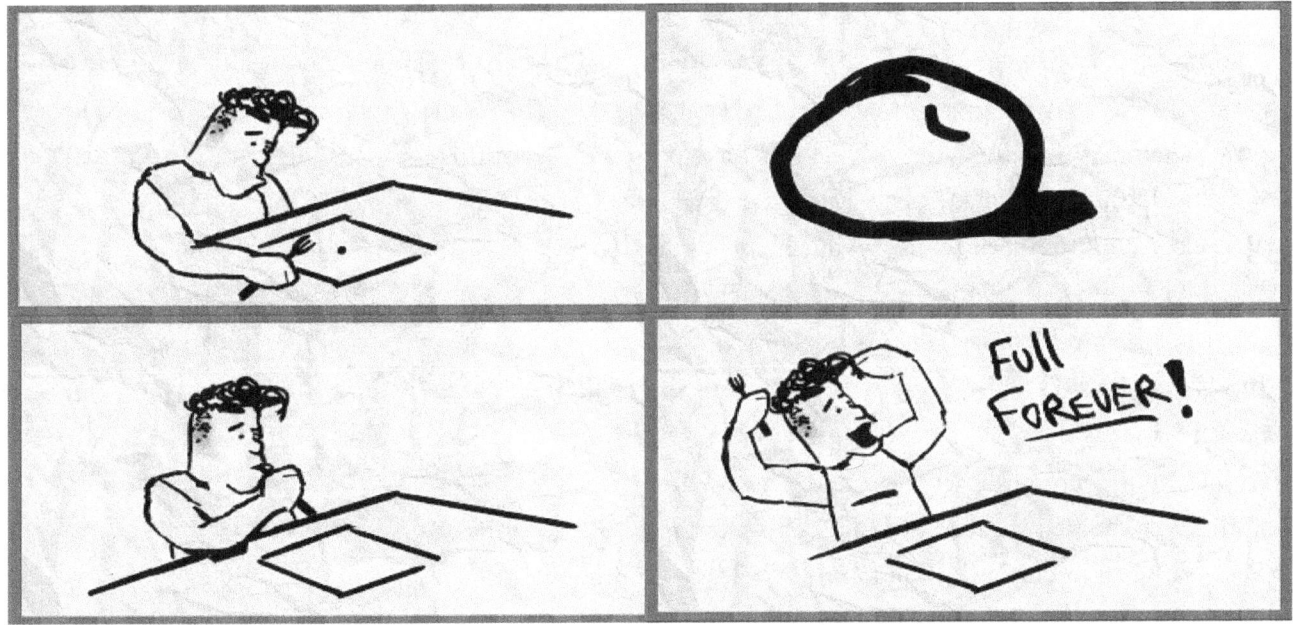

While commercials promote an irrational fear around that forever hungry feeling we have, self-help books cash in on our fears by perpetuating the mythos of an *inadequate, inauthentic identity* that needs fixing to keep us feeling *alive* (with hunger).

HUNGER IS THE EVIDENCE OF LIFE.

No wonder we are in such emotional turmoil in this commercial century! This is not to say that we are never in need of help out of the trenches of our traumas. We do often need help getting past our traumas; but who we fundamentally *are* does not need a doctor. As the saying goes, *the doctor gets paid so long as the patient stays sick.* Without sickness, it would be nonsense to train up doctors and priests. Then the pope could hock his white dress for a real ball gown!

Selling us the idea that the forever hungry feeling we have is a *new, unnatural problem* and that it needs fixing by opening up our mind (and our wallets!) is as ridiculous as teaching that happiness is *only* found by digging holes in the sky and selling you the shovel.

The myth of inherent soul sickness has created a pandemic of those who binge, but are never satisfied, and those who purge, but are never cleansed. Ever see a 3yr old running around with our first world kind of problems? Constantly worried about getting a bigger toy? Or a bigger diaper? Or whether they can afford to take a poop in brand name jeans? Of course not!

When you grasp for a cure to a sickness that's *not yours,* you are condemned to eternal zombie-like grasping because being well and being sick has become one and the same. Were we to wake up from this sickness of *inadequate identity*, entire industries would roll over to our new found power of non-participation.

You'd recognize your "I" has always *already* been whatever you needed or wanted "I" to be in the moment, even if that were a series of compromises. *Nothing is wrong.*

THE CAKE IS A LIE.

There *is* no carrot to chase to get to your true identity. The bag of goodies you are missing is entirely already *you.* It may be desirable or undesirable to you (and that is okay too!) but it has not drifted *anywhere* and is not any *less* "you". People have passed on from this life without *ever* unfurling 100% of their identity. And that's okay. But what if you *did*?

Who else can know the secrets of your heart better than you? I have yet to meet one person who reached *inward* only to come away empty handed. Although, what we find is not as forthcoming as a 'drive around to the second window'.

We have betrayed our hearts. We have chastised our true desires and shamed the identity that lights the fire in our eyes. We must apologize and hold an unyielding embrace

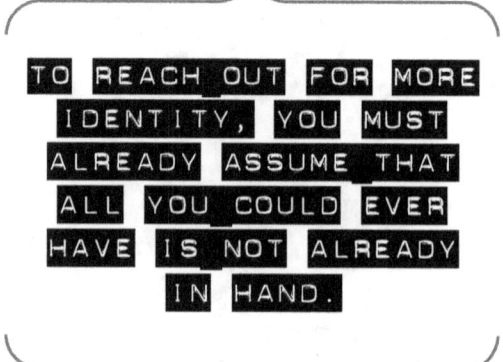

TO REACH OUT FOR MORE IDENTITY, YOU MUST ALREADY ASSUME THAT ALL YOU COULD EVER HAVE IS NOT ALREADY IN HAND.

in the *goodness* of the mystery that is "I" *until* our heart floods with our love and belief in it's *unknown* and our mystery rises to the surface. A heart that is filled with unedited self embrace will spill its deepest, most authentic and beautiful secrets.

When I tell people this shortcut to the "Path of Enlightenment", they look at me as though I am crazy. It's understandable. I would be peeved to find out I'd wasted a massive amount of time chasing an identity that really only existed, in its entirety, as a concept between the ears.

But it's true. Everything you will ever know about yourself is already within your grasp.

When is the time ever "good enough" to embrace your identity in it's *entirety,* seen and unseen? If not now, then when?

If identity were a tangible thing, it would function as such. We could find it, lose it, or destroy it. But identity is merely an *idea* we have about ourselves, one that we too often make a nightmare rather than a *dream come true.*

If identity were an *actual* thing, we could measure it and say, "Aha! Mine is smaller than *yours.* It is *inadequate.*" But, since "I" is one of those intangible things we've created for us *alone,* I can hit *refresh* whenever I grow bored or tired of how I play "me".

Even the least successful person in the world is adequate without *doing* anything.

Furthermore, your identity is nothing of itself, but is in the likeness of *anything* fundamentally *meaningful to you.* This is why I firmly believe,

I AM A UNICORN.

I find it easy to explain the paradox of my identity as a Unicorn, since they are:

- Both seen *and* have yet to be seen. Just like this fundamental 'me' I continually unfold.
- Unicorns are eternal *and* the figment of my imagination. As am "I".
- 'Unicorn' is heard by all, yet seen by none. As is every description of 'me'.
- Unicorns are something which many admire, yet none can quite grasp, which is also how people are around someone who is their authentic Self. And finally,

- Unicorns are an ambassador of two worlds: the magical and the ordinary, which is also how I feel when asked to explain my Self. I feel I'm being asked to explain my delight in my own madness.

You may be wondering, "But how do I solve the problem of when people around me feel threatened by my identity and think their identity is the only one that is *real*?"

The answer is: *Don't Bother*.

IT'S NOT YOUR PROBLEM.

Your job is to share what *you* love. They don't *have* to love you back.

As for those who feel threatened? Smile at them. Let them know you are *happy*. Don't subject yourself to them or the 'burden of proof' they seek to unload on you. That is *their* burden to carry.

And to those who go as far as question your very right to *exist*:

Hire them, but don't work for them.

Sell to them, but don't buy from them.

Offer lodging, but don't live under the same roof.

Then they see you do well *without* solving their problem, they will feel less obliged to obstruct your path or loot you for the insolvent riddle:

"If you are *you*, then who am I? What does that make me?"

Don't worry yourself with their troubles. Using corrosive logic (such as "If-thus-so") on a magical thing like identity will create a pathological *virus* of the mind: A conversational itch that can't be scratched. There is no causal effect- and no consequence- of crossing paths with someone's identity, so *why worry?* Take the wisdom of a child: Always *discover* the people around you.

When people appear to you, *celebrate*. Accept their appearance as a child would: Without doubt. They *are what they say they are*.

A child does not say to a stranger, "You *shouldn't* be here. You should not exist." But as adults, we can send that rejection and bitterness energetically to the *undiscovered* people around us. Don't be mean to people just because you don't understand them. They may share something profound about Life that you would otherwise *never know*.

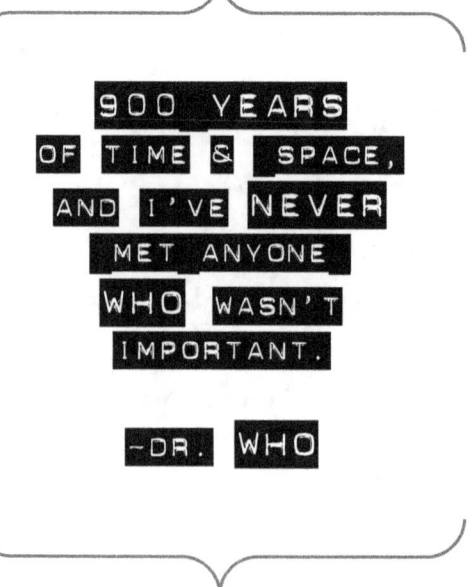

900 YEARS OF TIME & SPACE, AND I'VE NEVER MET ANYONE WHO WASN'T IMPORTANT.

-DR. WHO

Helen Keller is a great example of what language makes possible for our identity. Helen was blind and deaf by the time she could crawl, but because of the loving determination of her teacher, she learned to communicate by signing letters into the palm of the hand. "Before I had *words*," she signed, "I was a formless lump of *unfeeling* clay."

As a young child, and without the ability to communicate, Helen kicked and screamed whenever someone tried to control her incoherent behaviors. It is a real mystery how she never recalled *feeling* anything! Every action was a reaction: a fumbled response to outside stimuli. Her noises went without orchestration, which made for no music (no *meaningfulness*). Without words, Helen drifted. Nothing held her attention beyond the impulses: *Hunger, thirst, touch*. In fact, when asked to describe her experience, Helen said that she remembered almost *nothing* before her *first* word at eight years old.

How is that possible?

Is language the catalyst for *human* identity?

Is my identity merely the emotions from a *meaningful* interpretation of my life?

Is the amount of identity I have related to the amount of language that is available to me?

The DNA of [gender] identity is, in fact, meaningful descriptions through language. And where expansive language abounds, *watch out*! Gender and Identity *also* abound.

Ever wonder why there are cultures with 4 or 5 genders? *Their use of meaningful language.*

I remember the moment I realized the limitlessness of my gender identity.

I was overhearing a teacher speak to a group of LGBT youth,

"How do you know what *my* gender is?" He asked.

"By what you're wearing?" One guessed.

No.

"By how (long) you wear your hair?"

No.

"By which pronouns you use?"

No.

No? The room became still with thought.

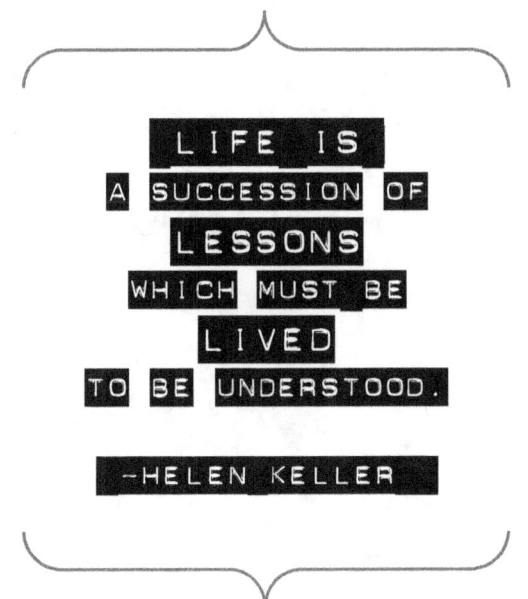

LIFE IS A SUCCESSION OF LESSONS WHICH MUST BE LIVED TO BE UNDERSTOOD.

-HELEN KELLER

"By what you *tell us* it is?" One boy said, sarcastically grinning.

"Exactly!" The teacher cheered. "For you to know what my gender is, I have to <u>*tell you*</u>."

That's when I realized: *Identity only exists in our ability to express our meaningfulness through language.*

Do you know what this means?

'I' is a creation of my own description.

The quality and quantity of my 'I' which exists in *your* world is only limited by my ability to communicate it to you.

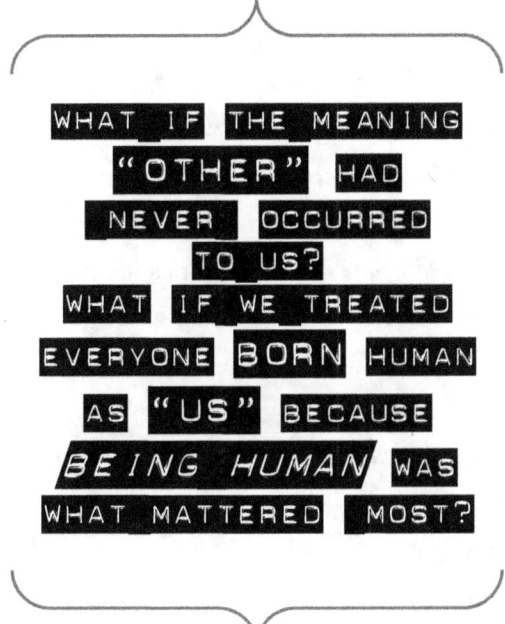

WHAT IF THE MEANING "OTHER" HAD NEVER OCCURRED TO US? WHAT IF WE TREATED EVERYONE BORN HUMAN AS "US" BECAUSE *BEING HUMAN* WAS WHAT MATTERED MOST?

New words organize our emotions and concepts. Words are a focal lens to give our emotions definition. In fact, our fundamental identity eludes us until we are mindful enough to *feel* it.

This doesn't mean you need big words, it simply means you need *self-awareness*.

What is self-awareness like?

Many things.

Your soul *delights* to be acknowledged by *you*.

Let me give you an example of how *words* allow us to *feel* and share our identity,

FOR ANYONE LGBT:

Consider that "Aha!" moment when you *first* connected that what you felt was both "gay" and "*love*". Suddenly, *there* it was: A distinct *form* of being never *felt* before! The words in the acronym "LGBT" represent nations of courageous people acknowledging who they are, *together*.

And together, we reached into our Selves and pull out *beautiful* forms of identity.

FOR ANYONE NOT LGBT:

Before you knew the word "transgender", it may not have occurred to you. Then one day, *voila!* "Transgender" becomes something real and tangible. We feel uncertain and concerned when we *can't* imagine how it must feel to be someone else. After all, the problem is: you *really* don't know what a trans person is experiencing *until you ask them*.

If you want to know how to treat a trans person, bring a child who still believes that the world is *magical*.

After all, *getting to know you* is perfectly natural to play with children 3 years and under. The child won't even notice someone is *not magical* until an adult breaks it to them and shatters their faith in people.

And even then, the child usually *gets* it when someone explains how they are *magically* gendered.

This is the wisdom that children bring to our conversations. *Play nice together. It is always worth your time to listen to who I am.*

Children *accept* transgender people as a part of our naturally magical world, because it follows what we've taught them: Balloons go *up,* rocks go *down,* and princesses get trapped by *enchantments*. It follows that a certain quiet boy just *might* be a loud and happy girl *waiting to be let out of her tower.* Children *want* you to get your happy ending. They *want* everyone's dream to come true, *not* just the normal *boring* ones. Children love and accept transgender people for who they *really are*: Lovable

IDENTITY ONLY EXISTS IN LANGUAGE, THEREFORE, I AM A CREATION OF MY OWN DESCRIPTION.

people who are magically growing into themselves, just like *children do*, but as adults.

The first thing I wanted to be when I grew up was a lion. That is, until my Sunday school teacher told me that I could *never* be one, because that *doesn't happen.* We teach children to treat *everyone's* feelings as *valid* and *worthy of their attention* until we (adults) convince them that their *own* feelings are *wrong.* When children aren't allowed to feel something because *someone else* determines it's bad or wrong, the magic dies. When we teach children to disregard their own feelings, their feelings for others form unhealthy codependence and reflect their desire to self-harm.

To many LGBT people, this moment of rejecting their own emotions galvanizes their entire approach to their identity, too often, even into adulthood.

And whatever feelings you have about LGBT identity? It's okay!

Take as much time as you need. We'll *still* be LGBT when you figure things out.

And you are *definitely* not alone in this struggle. Starting conversations with NEW friends (not old ones) around your struggle can bring a fresh perspective to old objections. You have the right to feel safe with your own thoughts. If it helps, you can ask to sit down with a support group *without* having to participate in the discussion. I bet if you asked, *a loved one would even sit with you.* It may help you hear others who are *not LGBT* process their feels together. I've found many valuable friends through online support groups as well. Try searching your local area for a PFLAG (Parents, Friends, and Family of Lesbians and Gays)

.

IF YOU STILL HAVE NO IDEA
HOW WORDS ALLOW US TO FEEL AND SHARE OUR IDENTITY:

Do this exercise.

Take a gym whistle and a friend: Turn your friend so that their back is facing you.

Ask your friend to *guess* the emotion you are expressing with the whistle.

Try the emotion *love.*

Play that emotion on a whistle *without* speaking.

Lemme tell you, *it's difficult.*

Once your friend is done guessing, try to convey the feeling *anticipation.*

I actually enjoy playing a recording of this back to people. We are so immersed in our own emotion that we don't actually hear how *meaningless* we come off to everyone else.

Our emotions shout out before the words come. Most of us need a medium (canvas, instrument, keyboard, etc) to process our emotional identity into something *tangible.*

Don't leave home without an emotional medium.

In conclusion, if I am what I describe, then there's no logic in arguing with myself. There is no horror that *I* have not authored, no internal pressure that *I* have not placed there myself. If I don't like it, I have to take it up with *me.* In my head, there is neither good nor evil. There is merely what is desirable and what is undesirable to me.

With all choices, there are only two outcomes:

A. Greater connections

B. Greater suffering

Both are appropriate in their own circumstance. I believe that the outcome of my choice may even *change* based on the time that decision is made. I feel our core identity lets us struggle in this way. No natural birth is done without difficulty. Those choices that bring us close to ourselves unearth our core power identity. An imbalance in energy exchange between us and others can result in a whirlwind affect: enhancing *them* while uprooting our sense of Self. This is something that can happen gradually or immediately.

Ever been afraid of speaking the truth because what it will do? Ever wonder why?

Speaking the truth cuts false time lines from of our path. False time lines are places, people, and things who entangle us and weigh us down on our path. Telling the truth removes their entanglements and allows us to move on. Your truth allows you to change the entire landscape of your life, and *always* for the better. Even if people resist it, the truth will take them out of your life and give you a place you freely belong. Follow your truth.

Has telling the truth ever gotten you fired?

Good! Have you ever noticed that afterward, you felt relieved? Like suddenly, *you can breathe.*

You've been *enlightened.*

YOUR TRUTH IS YOUR POWER IDENTITY. USING IT CREATES A WORMHOLE IN TIME: PULLING YOU THROUGH ANYTHING OR ANYONE, AT ANYTIME.

FOLLOW THE WHITE RABBIT

And you're back on your path! Be proud! No one has ever died from being fired. It only *feels* like our life is over, but we can always turn it around.

It can almost feel like our "failures" were actually doing us a *favor.* That's because the truth removes pieces of time (things/places) that *don't belong* because it is cluttering us up from:

A. Telling the truth

B. Loving ourselves, or

C. Stopping us along our path.

Ever lost your house because you told the truth of who you are? Good! Be glad for it!

You are the lucky one. You've unloaded a burden and you're back on your path!

NEVER STOP TELLING YOUR TRUTH.

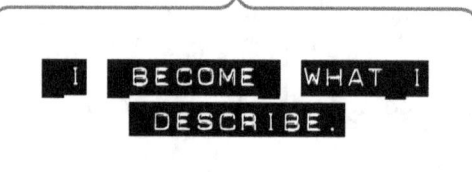

I BECOME WHAT I DESCRIBE.

We see the truth threatens to change our lives *because it does,* and in a good way. The truth is a knife that cuts through the bullshit. Shaping self-fondness through expressing your truth allows you to come away with as much peace and pleasure as you can carry. I'm calling you to that change, not by force, but by self-observation.

Observe yourself. Give yourself the same emotional considerations you would with your dearest friend. Don't blame yourself for everything. Be empathetic like you would to a kid whose been bullied all his life. Only this kid is *you.* And *the bully* is you, also.

Apologize if you need to.

When I feel depressed, I imagine walking into the very same room in which I'm seated and seeing my very best friend laying here in my place, beating themselves up. I would *know* how to console them and what would make them feel better.

And I then do that for myself.

I look out for my best friend. I say things in a kinder matter and I console them. I express to them how sorry I am that they're in pain and, even though I have no answers, I pledge my love is with them. I listen to what they cry about and I cry *with them.* If I can do that for someone else, why not be that listening friend for *myself?* Don't I hurt sometimes? And don't I sometimes need understanding and sincere condolence?

People show a *myriad* of ways to embrace their identity, but don't get caught up in all the words words words.

What matters is that you are using *your* voice to speak truths to *yourself.*

You DO care about you, otherwise you would forget to breathe.

So why not go *all out?* Why not be your *favorite soul?* "You" as your favorite of all friends and lovers? Spoil *you* with kindness!

What is the *worst* that could happen?

People becoming jealous of what you share with yourself?

A madly *loved* identity is so powerful, it should come with its own warning label.

IDENTITY AS ART

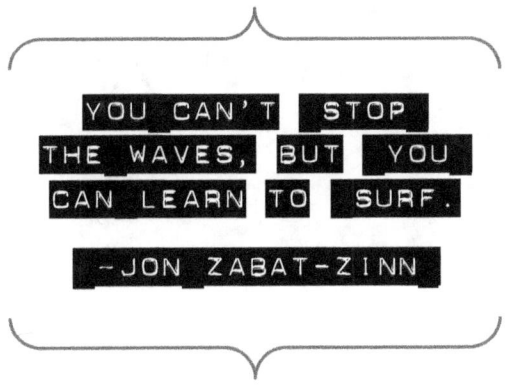

YOU CAN'T STOP THE WAVES, BUT YOU CAN LEARN TO SURF.

-JON ZABAT-ZINN

Just as wind is produced when something is in motion, your identity is produced whenever you are emotionally *moved*. The "I" in identity is our oldest expression of Art. What I'm talking about here is the art of the imagination, when we first made things *beautiful* through *meaningfulness*. Art is not just in painting and sculptures, but art is in First, Middle, and Last names, the ways clothes hang on our bodies, and the movements we use to indicate our sex and our desire for social interaction.

This and a myriad of other behaviors are an *art* to us. Whenever we find someone "not playing by the rules" we all experience a moment of unidentifiable fear.

The fear that our game can't control what is *real...* because it *can't*: It's not real *either*.

I once had the opportunity to witness how art became identity, and thus made this identity an expression of that *art form*.

I told my friend to ask a cute boy out I'd seen at the mall. Their response?

"Oh. He's a Hollister boy."

I stared blankly.

"He's a Hollister boy," my friend repeated, "They're boys who only wear Hollister clothes *and* go out with those who only wear Hollister."

"That's- that's a *thing*?" I stuttered.

I looked around... "Well," I said, "I suppose someone had to start this whole 'wearing clothes' thing. Probably stopped dating boys in the nude." I smirked.

"That's probably what got us to where we are now." My friend laughed.

The game of Hollister boys is equally as potent as any other. If you solicit *enough* people to play it, an identity can take on a life of its own; like my story of giraffes.

I could tell you in intricate detail the activities, colors, conversations, postures, and decorations I may hang on my body in order to play the role of a *binary* sex and no one would second guess my authenticity. But, I am horrified that no one is unsettled by what these little binary (male/female) rituals cost of our *internal spark*. If you miss feeling alive, dress as something entirely different.

It makes little difference to me when someone (especially someone who is *not* me) hurls insults at my qweird (queer+weird) identity and "art".

Seriously! What fool screams that art is *wrong*?

Art is neither wrong *nor* true, thus the point of creating one's identity is to *enjoy* what you have created, to change at will, and in mastering change: Master the boundaries of Self.

The only one who can say is "I";

LANGUAGE IS POWER

When you quit something in your life, it is essential to *replace it* with something else. This is because the brain cannot tell between reality and thoughts of reality. When you think of *not* doing something, the brain fires in *the same way* as if you are *doing that very thing*. This makes it impossible for the mind to work in anti-thought.

Let me illustrate an example:

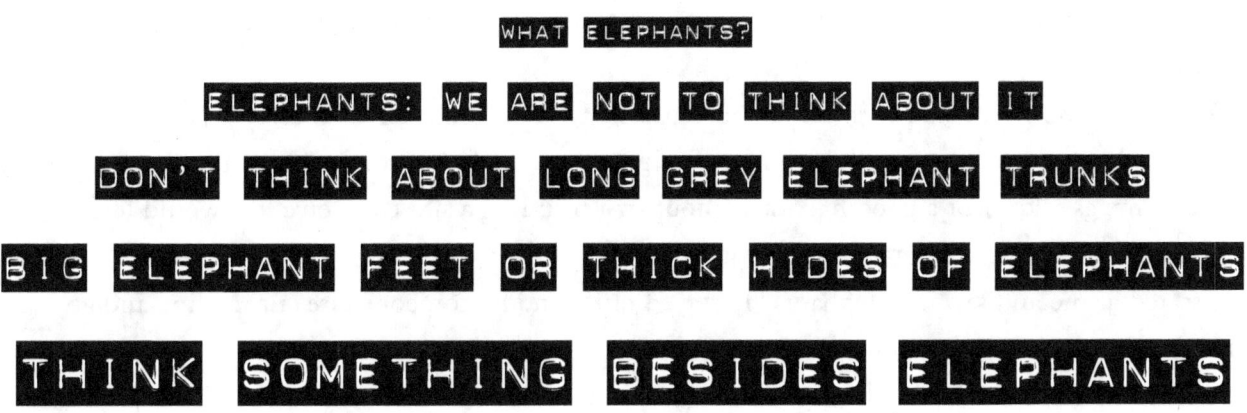

Now, what were we just thinking of?

ELEPHANTS?

See? The mind cannot work in *Anti-thought*.

The funniest thing about using language is watching other people be unable to avoid the things you create. With a single meaningful word, I can shift a conversation in any direction I choose and without permission. This makes for one magical mother fucking identity!

I've known some people whose identity even took on anti-hero vibe: Identifying as things for which they are *against*. I've found that they were equally puzzled by their ineffectiveness to move the world as they accidently, continually creating that thing for which they were stubbornly *against* with their language.

Take one example of abortion protestors. It was interesting to observe them a few years back. The more they talked about the problems of abortions, the more the crowd only talked about abortion. It became clear to me the conversation left a vacuum around alternatives. Even pro-choicers readily offered alternatives. One of the protestors, a Christian by profession, prayed loudly for God to end abortion. I waited for him to finish before approaching him.

"What do you propose then as an alternative to abortion?" I asked, "What would you have?"

He answered, "Alternatives? Well, like adoption."

"Oh? So you have adopted some children, then?" I smiled, "How many?"

He looked at me at first with surprise. His look of confusion soured.

I waited, but the silence yawned. He looked at me, frowning. I looked at him, a student in front of a teacher.

"How many children have you taken in?" I asked again.

"I don't have *any* children." He said flatly.

I looked at him confused. "If they are not with *you*, then where do they go?"

"There are plenty of foster homes."

"Where?"

"Hm?"

"Where? I don't know of any, do you? Which foster home do you take these children?"

He turned back to the line up to the stage. I stood and waited with him, but he stayed quiet and looked away.

"What about you?" He said with a clouded expression, "You adopt any babies?"

"Well, as I have no home myself," I confessed, "praying to end abortion would make about as much sense to me as asking for a good harvest without first building a silo to receive it. I would feel ungrateful to the one who granted my request."

He stared at me and saw the elephant. He stayed quiet and let someone else cut the line and go ahead of him, contemplated my dilemma.

Our conversation dissolved as he took the stage, but the kindness in his voice rose above the crowd as I slipped back into the grey.

Understand. No one is going to give their baby away to someone who thinks they are rescuing them from their filthy incompetent mothers. Many more women would choose adoption if they were saturated with realistic and considerate options. Imagine how far a $10 phone card could go if attached to a list of people waiting to take care of them during their pregnancy and adopt their baby, if *they* chose them?

People are smart. Women are smart. They *want* to believe the world can be kinder for them and their children. But most people need someone to have the courage to step into that reality *for* them. That is: If you want to make a world of difference, *believe in someone else's greatness.*

If you want someone to come unstuck from a difficult path, you have to believe in that person's greatness and consistently create opportunities for them, no matter the outcome. People don't want to be liked for compromising. They want to be respected, regardless if they participate or not.

Everyone wants to do things that inspire us and others, we just sometimes only see that brokenness is our reality.

Now I know what you're thinking: What about mom? Every time she *breathes* she tells me how I'm _____.

There's no way to kill an 'idea' of *you* in someone else's head, but there are entertaining ways to ninja your way out of someone's presumptions about you. We all know someone who believes we are _____ and decided we're gonna *stay that way*. Like mother. She shares who (she thinks) we are, as if that's *all there is*. But does mother always knows best?

I didn't see my mom's words as a creative force in my life until I was much older. When she launches an old identity in my direction now, I enjoy it, as she does so to her own unicorn's *peril*.

I start by amusing myself with mother's crazy-making. Rather than getting all chewed up by her accusations, I dress up in her darkest nightmares of my 'self' and play out my 'villainy' in the *most* ridiculous and/or obscene fashion *possible*. If mother *thinks* I'm part of the 'gay agenda', I make it my game to remove *all* doubt. For example: I'd pass rainbow candy out to all the grandkids before offering her some *only* if she pledges to be *gay* for a day, as if that is what I had been doing all along. And let the fun begin!

When mom lists why I'm undesirable or inadequate, I quickly derail the conversation to how poorly she has underestimated me. *I'm so much more tacky and overestimated than she ever imagined, and worst yet, I enjoy every moment of it!* Not only will she kill her own unicorn conversation to escape the joke that is now on *her*, but she'll also hesitate to produce more assumptions about me next time, lest I slay her unicorns in my wake!

If I'm exactly who I created (whether good/ugly/right/wrong/indifferent) and my mother deems it as *less* valuable, I must first agree that my identity has *any value* to her *in the first place*. My identity is clearly *not* hers to begin with. Living under a hijacked identity so that mother doesn't have to face her demons is *ridiculous*! Especially when "I" is so worthy to *feel alive*!

Why not disarm motherly accusations with inclusive humor rather than oppose her with an equal dose of rejection? After all, it's their isolation from qweirdos like us that keeps them so cold. I prefer to pile on all the crazy in *their* corner and let it smoke'em out. Let me give you an example of one such conversation:

MOM: "You're waist is getting too big."
ME: (What I think) too big is so lackluster. I could be a fat fat fat whale of a bearded lady! What a grand pirate I would make!
(What I actually say) …Okay *mom*. I get that you are saying that my waist is not desirable to you,

MOM: -No I'm not...

ME: (delighted) Oh good! Then we agree I'm perfect!

MOM: -I just think you're waist could be smaller.

ME: (Thinking) If I were perceived as a man, I could be any size that I wanted.

(What I say) Actually mother, this is the only waist I have and it's *this* size; and I can hate it or I can love it, but it *only* comes in this size today.

MOTHER: (Laughs) Well. You can make it *smaller*.

ME: Got a knife?

MOTHER: You know that's *not* what I meant!

ME: Actually you do, mom... Or would you rather I hurt myself *very slowly*, so as not to upset anyone? So I can fit your ideal pants? Well I say: let's quicken the pace mom! Where's the knife?

MOM: You're Crazy!

ME: (Grinning) I know! I just love this *fat* body so much! It so fucking fantastic! See! I can have all the fun that I *want*!

MOM: ... (Rolls eyes and looks around for help)

ME: (says) Let's see them skinny bitches having this much fun!

(thinking) *Nailed it!*

Best advice I give when fighting a unicorn is: Play out their *obscene* logic to its own insane end. In other words, agree to dance with it and dance it right off a cliff. People will literally kill their own Unicorn concepts to escape the horror and mystery that is in the *magic* of *you*. Seriously. Go on. Another approach to rendering an overly obnoxious Unicorn in power, such as a boss you must pussy foot around, is to internally acknowledge the illogical perspective they are pitching and its lack of any *actual* value to *you*.

What mom or my boss thinks has absolutely *nothing* to do with me. It's not my problem.

I'm equally as cautious with compliments as I'm with curses from them, as someone of *any* value can be misled to believe they have been *devalued*.

However, *my logic is*:

- Since there is only one person that is *me*,

- And there is no one quite as magnificently nuanced, quite as scarred, quite as clever, or quite as brassy,

- And there is *no one* I can compare myself to other than an imaginary me I think I *should* be. A me, no doubt, taken from a compilation of other people, all of whom are *not* me.

There's therefore *no* sense in placing an "inherent value" on any comparison to me. Comparing myself to *anyone* else is pure vanity, as they would fail miserably at being *me*.

Thus, when people retch up a unicorn that I am *not* prepared to entertain, I throw it into the pile of "idea's that are not actually *for* or *about* me", and move on.

If you want to open an air hole in the conversational ceiling, don't aim at the head. Most people don't understand their own programming, and you can't unprogram someone by telling them they are *wrong* or their creations have no actual value, because their thoughts are *not wrong,* they're just not what *you* wanted or expected to hear.

The best thing to say when someone makes a judgment about you is a sincere, "Ok! (I can see that)," Dance with the madness that is our identity and constantly remind yourself how *ridiculous* we all sound! Especially when pretending we are heralds of the 'important things in life'. These are often the most detrimental advice we have on hand!

The whole point of identity is to *enjoy* it. Whether "I" is simple or complex, made for admiration or derision--- if you aren't *absolutely* in love with what you've created— you are a sad creation indeed.

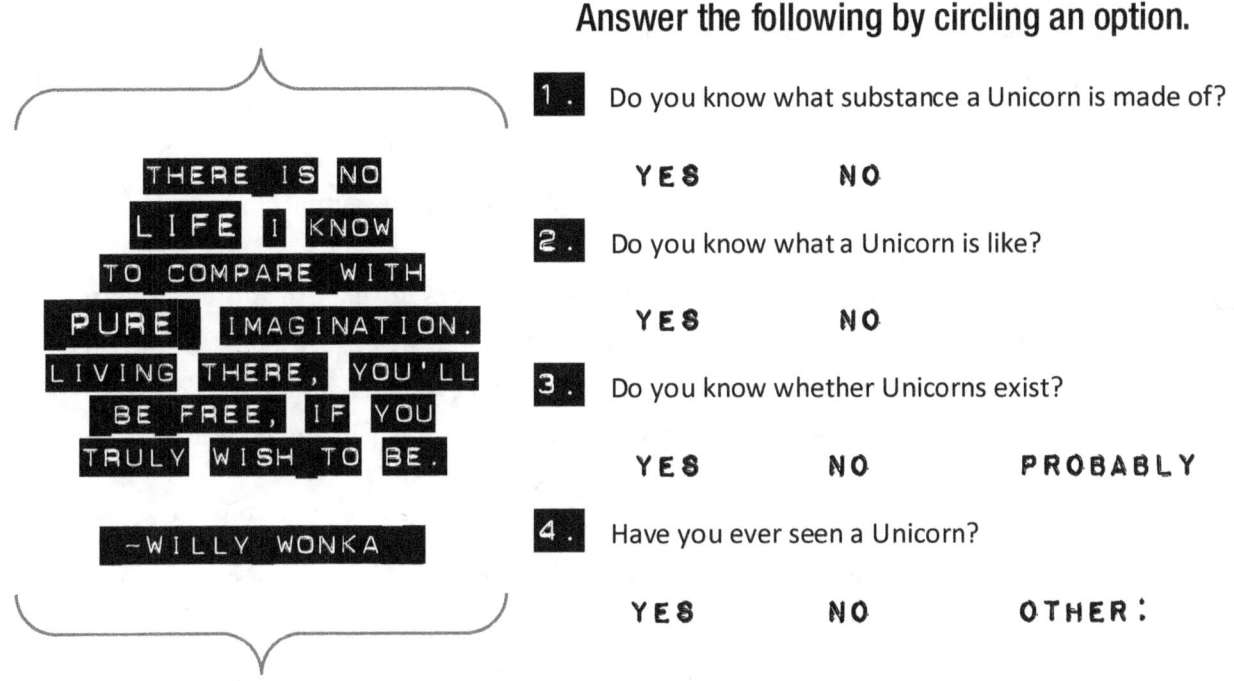

Answer the following by circling an option.

1. Do you know what substance a Unicorn is made of?

YES   NO

2. Do you know what a Unicorn is like?

YES   NO

3. Do you know whether Unicorns exist?

YES   NO   PROBABLY

4. Have you ever seen a Unicorn?

YES   NO   OTHER:

THERE IS NO
LIFE I KNOW
TO COMPARE WITH
PURE IMAGINATION.
LIVING THERE, YOU'LL
BE FREE, IF YOU
TRULY WISH TO BE.

~WILLY WONKA

This is a personality test to determine if you've got what it takes to develop your *own* gender identity: A feisty imagination.

Let me explain. First, you have to understand: Unicorns actually *do* exist.

Yes they do.

If unicorns didn't exist, how would you know what one was?

Someone had to tell you. (Sound familiar?)

"Unicorn" is a meaningful word. And from that word came stories and images and legends. From one word, a nation of "unicorn" manifested, leaping from a thousand words and a thousand storybooks. There are many tricky concepts like the Unicorn which lay hidden in our language. The most obvious being:

I · DEN · TI · TY

Identity is also like the Unicorn, in that:

- You don't know what gender identity consists of, yet you think it's *real*.

- You can discover more of what identity is *like*, but no one can say what it *actually is*.
  (This is why adult's shrug when you ask who they will be when they grow up.)

- You don't know when your identity will be finished changing.
  (Let me save you the time by saying *never-* unless you've given up.)

- Your identity will always expand in proportion to your ability to express it in meaningful ways.

Like unicorns, your identity was born from the imagination through language. And like unicorns, your identity has elements of being both unreal and having actual effect on people. Kind of like a delightful madness.

I find that identity creates a curious lapse in logic. It's sometimes difficult to address because people who feel their identity is threatened will emotionally shut down without even knowing *why*. On the other hand, if you perceive your identity as intangible, you'll also realize its *untouchable*. Understanding identity this way can make navigating your identity around other's objections both entertaining and enlightening.

Identity, including that of gender, is merely a paintbrush with unlimited amounts of both meaningful and meaningless applications. Someone's fundamental identity doesn't have to be an emotional experience for you. However, gender and identity are so often *deeply* meaningful to others, that treating their fundamental identity with regard will almost always insure a mutually respectful and beneficial encounter in conversation.

If someone's identity doesn't suit you, just remember: It not supposed to. It's *their* identity. Often, playing with gender appears either mystical or mad to people around you.

In either case, it's no cause for concern. My length of hair or apparel does not impede your ability to function.

Stop policing gender and identity! Then others will suddenly come to *life* around you. Disregard your family and friend's obligation to appease your imaginary friends, "Right" and "Order", and you'll suddenly find you are *both* free to be exactly who you delight in the *most*. Gender Atheists are some of the most beautiful, free, happy people I know. They are not attached to any one identity, gender, or social pressure to appear as anything other than what they truly enjoy being at the moment.

You can pretend Identity exists and Unicorns don't, but we still proliferate our language to fit our limitless Self into a spray of cartoonish stereotypes. We all secretly acknowledge that words are never *enough* to completely describe us. But, as our descriptions for our identity multiplies, our identities also multiply. For example: the

U·NI·TY

INCLUSION THROUGH CELEBRATED DISTINGUISHED DIFFERENCES, AS OPPOSED TO EXTINGUISHING THOSE DIFFERENCES. (SEE FASCISM)

"Queer" community later became the "Gay" and "Lesbian" community, which later became "Butch/Femme", "Gender Queer", "Agendered", "Intergendered", "Trans" and so on and so on. There is no true way for a person to know your gender identity without you first telling (i.e. creating) it for them. It is this mindfulness of yourself as the creator that frees you up to first become detached from other's ideas about you, and then go on to create your *favorite* Self; making you both the delighting creator and our delighted creation, together.

Therefore, identity is a unicorn, which both does and does not exist; As we both create it while we pretend as though we are being auto-created by some external force other than our Selves. Creating delight through identity is the moral of life's story, and like any story, we've simply complicated it to the point that no one is delighting in themselves because no one *belongs*. This has created the misery and loneliness inside of us: A myriad of identity problems are born from believing we must moralize (i.e. 'make right') our imagined Self to fit an external imaginary stereotype or standard.

As if what we think of ourselves *could* be wrong? Or even *real*?

Nonsense! This pathologic obsession with unity through extinguishing *difference* is the root of human anguish. For how can one make what is already healthy *healthy* again? You can't. You first have to make it ill.

If you realize that there is no standard, no boundary, no omniscient force dramatizing your Self reflection, you can always seek to exert the wellness you *already have* over your whole Self.

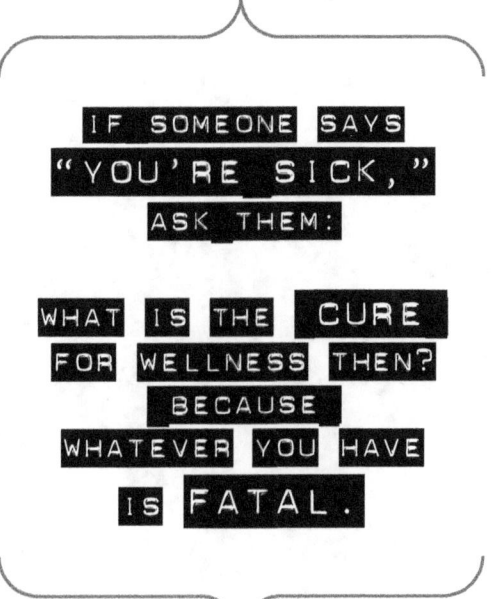

IF SOMEONE SAYS "YOU'RE SICK," ASK THEM: WHAT IS THE CURE FOR WELLNESS THEN? BECAUSE WHATEVER YOU HAVE IS FATAL.

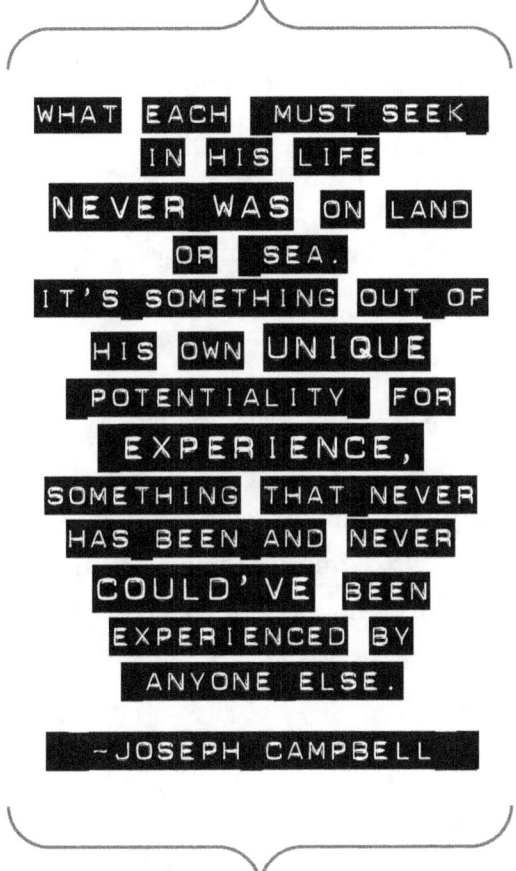

WHAT EACH MUST SEEK
IN HIS LIFE
NEVER WAS ON LAND
OR SEA.
IT'S SOMETHING OUT OF
HIS OWN UNIQUE
POTENTIALITY FOR
EXPERIENCE,
SOMETHING THAT NEVER
HAS BEEN AND NEVER
COULD'VE BEEN
EXPERIENCED BY
ANYONE ELSE.

~JOSEPH CAMPBELL

Remember this about other people's moral "standards": If they created it, let them enjoy the monster! Who are you to stand in their way?

If someone calls themselves "fat" or says "god hates fags", I acknowledge their statement with an "Ok! (I see that)". A strong statement about life is nothing less than the plea to *see* what they see.

It is to this I agree. I see what they see. I observe their statement without offense, that is, I acknowledge them as an observer, a non-participant.

Conflict is heavy. It is no fun to fight when there is no one to fight against. "I'm right/you're wrong" is a tedious ego driven game. When someone screams, "God hates fags!" I say, "Ok! (I see that)"

So what? They may hate me, but there is no logic in *arguing* whether god hates fags or the color purple is dangerous to kangaroos!

I was astonished to realize that by my very participation, I perpetuated the problem. As soon as I responded in opposition, I actually propped *up* the argument! And once I unwittingly enter into dialogue I found myself the emotional crash pad for people to spew their Unicorn objections at. Ugh!

On the other hand, when I removed myself as *their* obstacle, and with no one to oppress, these same people become weighed down with their own Unicornstupation. You can kill a unicorn by starving the conversation out.

As I continue to create dialogue around being one's true self and allowing others to be whatever they want (whether desirable or undesirable to me) it becomes easy to handle strong idealists without feeling overwhelmed. Why? Because I'm only personally invested in observing others while I evolve my sense of self. I can participate in a peaceful inquiry on the meaning in life or kindly observe a strong statement *without* participating. No matter what the idea, the person is not talking about me. They are telling me about *themselves*. They want me to see who they are, as if that is all there is. It is freeing when your desire to be seen is compassionately acknowledged. In this way we are all one and the same.

Now, there are a few times worth noting where the person took a violent stance against me with the sole purpose of injuring me. In this moment, if possible, I peacefully remove myself and stop participating in their presence *at all*. It is not worthy of my attention. I'm reminded that the conversation has nothing to *actually* do with me. This is because the argument was present in them before I even arrived. At this point, I state clearly and aloud (and repeatedly if it is brought up to me sometime later) that I choose not to participate in *their* conflict. This may also mean quietly removing myself from any environment that would target me for maniacal entertainment.

Don't take on a person's unicorn unless you *enjoy* doing so. If the joy has left, retire the conversation. You are here to observe and live, bouncing between the roles of "self" and "other". Don't despise a person's conversation. See it for what it is, and move on sister!

Here below, I've provided a list for you of all possible identities. I've labeled this my "List of Unicorns". It only appears blank because:

- All things are possible, and
- *None* of which are real, have any permanence, or any value *other than what you assign.*

And, because it has no inherent value, it can be changed immediately, without forethought or struggle. As soon as you write down your identity in this box, you also eliminate the possibility of your being anything *else* simultaneously, including its opposite. This is how I came to believe that living with a blank slate is best for a pliable, delicious, and limitless personality.

WHAT IS YOUR IDENTITY LIKE?

I admit that creating your own (self-creating) identity can sometimes seem confusing, because I'm using words to describe to you what only exists in wordy language.

It feels like the eye looking back at itself. Hence, a repetitive looping in logic is inevitable.

This sort of looping is a telltale sign of a "unicorn" concept---- a thing which does *not* actually exist outside of language, a thing which has no actual value but lots of *meaning* attributed to it; a thing for which people may endlessly fight to solidify into fact, but will find a futile effort.

LIST OF UNICORNS

MY BODY

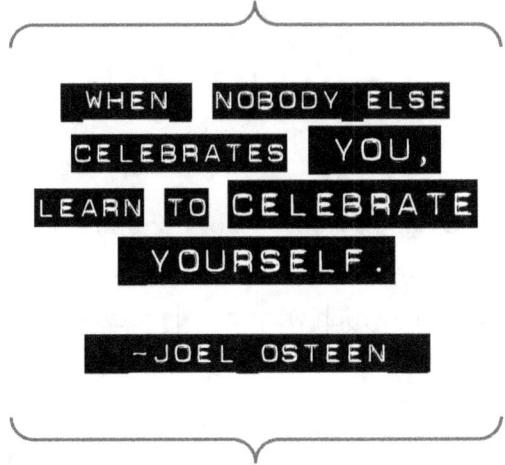

WHEN NOBODY ELSE CELEBRATES YOU, LEARN TO CELEBRATE YOURSELF.

-JOEL OSTEEN

I once changed jobs from a formal to an informal environment. Suddenly what I wore mattered very little. I took that opportunity to break out my tackle box of jewelry and gauged earrings. I called over my conservative Kansas boyfriend excitedly.

"No!" He seethed at my New Zealand fishhooks that dangled from each ear. "Take them out *now!*"

I realized this had truly been the first time he'd seen me punk out on my wardrobe. I was the embarrassing gay reflection of what he felt pressured to hide in public.

It was his patronizing command, however, that straightened my spine and set my teeth on edge.

"Let's get this straight *right now*," I flattened my jovial tone, "I didn't *ask* your permission."

I never seen a man ten years my senior humble himself so quick. He hadn't realized he'd made a gendered ass of himself.

"This is *my* body." I leveled with him as I took his tie in my hand. "I'll do whatever I want to it."

He stood still. I felt flush and my feet tingled. The hush that fell on the house sounded like a waterfall in my ears. I was a good 6" shorter than him, but he knew that I was the fearless sort of scrappy. That's what he liked about me.

"I've paid my dues. And it belongs to *me* now." I finished my thought and kissed his slightly frightened expression. After that, I never heard him tell me no again.

I can't count how many conversations I've had with women who've needed this very delicate principle of ownership. When I accept a lover, he/she/te is not a shareholder *buying* stock in my body or my identity. They are being given a finite opportunity to share a moment with me.

When I walk between two [gender] worlds, I'm often more fully aware of my own special power: A flexible Self that is just meant for *me*. "I" is flexible for *no one* but on behalf of my own pleasure. I protect my expansive emotional identity because it's what gives me unlimited access to what I need to be a healthy, well adjusted person.

My desire for equality requires that I continually announce myself until I am indistinguishable from the privileged. In that moment, I had immediately clarified my absolute sovereignty over my whole Self without intimidation, just as he had always safely assumed within the walls of *his* privilege. My declaration of independence disturbed him, as he'd never dealt with *anyone* (especially female) who loudly *owned* their body.

He'd always assumed his body (and by extension, my body,) was always his.

This confrontation shifted his perception of me to one who is self governed (master) rather than impetuous (subdued). The legendary weight of my gender mythos then saturated our conversations.

I became what I described to him.

In life, so long as my right to self-govern is in question, I will dutifully exercise my power to declare my Self *without* permission. If I had not taken a stand that day, I would have set a precedent with my lover. I would have accepted his idea of me as his subjugate property as he'd always unconsciously *assumed* of women/females, and comfortably slipped into the role he imagined himself: as my begrudging overseer.

I let him know I'd have none of that.

Our fatal mistake in obtaining equality is in announcing our separateness from it. For example: By demanding equal treatment, or complain in our constant state of *unequal*, we are confessing our separation and exclusion from the very thing we want- and- the thing which we can only seize in conversation.

I did not complain that was I treated unfairly, which would have only insured that I *accepted* that role. Instead, I leveled him. I seized back my power by declaring my identity as eye-level with his (and his privilege).

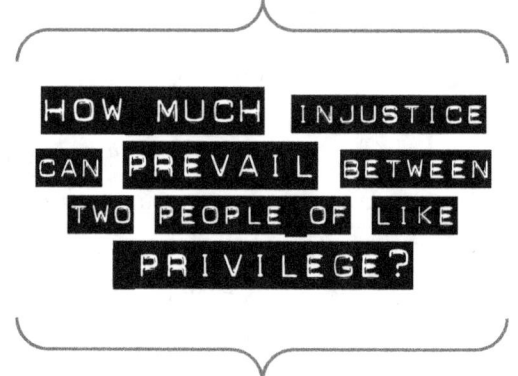

We may hack privileges by hack-tivating the language of it's masters. Mimicry is nature's way of gaining an advantage that would otherwise be unavailable. So why do we frequently speak about privilege as if we are still its illegitimate children? Pounding on the door of privilege to be let in? Surely this is what keeps us *outside*. It is not our sex or our color that segregate us any longer, but our slave language, our subdued body language, our permissiveness in the face of abuses, and our many wounded words expressing helplessness and resent. If we speak as their subjects, they will behave as our kings.

Seize every opportunity to sharpen your teeth on the language of kings. Master's have nothing to beg. The signature of the privileged is in their ability to cast a blind eye on those *under* them. Bend the lens of your identity with bold speech and you won't feel the pinch of discrimination or lost opportunities. That's why we need transgender people and those who can serve as a go-between, secretly infiltrating the highest levels of privilege and opening wide the front door of opportunity on those who are still knocking at its door.

We will only know we've reached equality when the language around our "differences" become less meaningful and that begins with *us*. What I wish is that we won't find a *use* for describing a human's color, gender, or sexuality *except* as we would describe it as we were *distinguishing a king*. When that happens, we will see wages for women improve. We will see two women together as just another *marriage*, and we no longer state "we're gay," but rather, "we're in love".

That is as close as we will ever know what living as equals will look like.

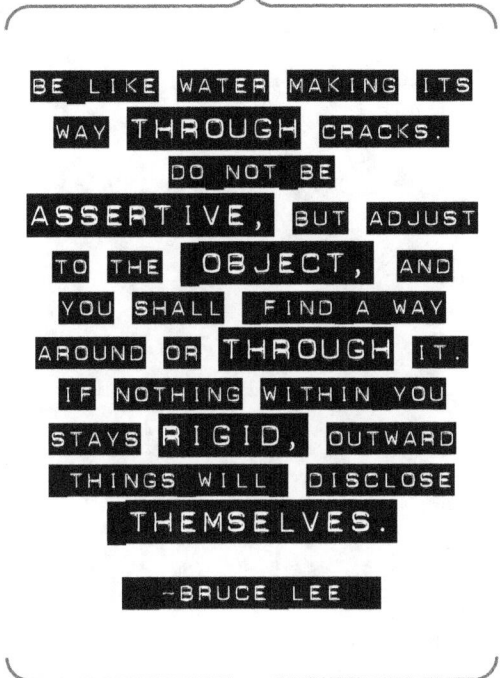

BE LIKE WATER MAKING ITS WAY THROUGH CRACKS. DO NOT BE ASSERTIVE, BUT ADJUST TO THE OBJECT, AND YOU SHALL FIND A WAY AROUND OR THROUGH IT. IF NOTHING WITHIN YOU STAYS RIGID, OUTWARD THINGS WILL DISCLOSE THEMSELVES.

-BRUCE LEE

November 21st, 2005:

I'd been looking to meet another transgender male for months. I had questions. *How did you do it? Where do you go for hormones? What can I expect?*

My heart was in my throat. People gathered in the cobble stone garden with their paper cupped candles as a man approached the stage, arm in arm with another man. "Today, we remember our people," he spoke softly at the pulpit.

Today was Transgender Day of Remembrance, our Dia de los Muertos (day of the dead) for transgender people. He beckoned us to look for the light in the darkness and to not forget those who died for us. The man next to him lit his candle and offered the first light to the crowd.

I had never been to a memorial for the dead.

A projector slowly scrolled names and locations of transgender people who had died that year. I waited impatiently, but the list made time stand still. The longer I stood there, the more it dawned on me:

The names never repeated.

I caught my breath. There were hundreds. As the light floated from candle to candle, lighting up this gathering in the courtyard, I wondered how many lights had floated away on dark nights like this. I heard voices around me as I stared in silence;

Gisberta, Porto, Portugal, Stoned to Death

Rani, Calcutta, Stoned To Death

Vanessa Facen, San Diego CA, "Stopped Breathing" while in the custody of police

Unknown, Northridge CA, dismemberment

Simone Walton, Dallas TX, Multiple shot wounds

Paulina (Juan Pablo) Mendez, Guatemala City, Shot to death by police

Alexis L. King, Nicetown PA, Shot To Death

Tiffany Berry, Memphis TN, Multiple Gunshot Wounds

Yardena Marsh, Tel Aviv, Israel, Multiple Gunshot Wounds

Mo Green, Phoenix AZ, Multiple Gunshot Wounds

Alfred Dibble, Stockton CA, Fatal beating to the head

Lakshmi, Tiruchy, India, Genital Mutilation

Geovanny Calderon, Guatemala City Guatemala, Multiple Gunshot Wounds

Divas B., Portage la Prairie, Manitoba CAN, Beaten to Death

Unknown , Long Beach CA, Beaten to Death

Unknown, Surco Peru, Incineration

Ryan Shey Hoski, Albuquerque NM, Undetermined; Signs of Upper Body Trauma

Penny Port Sheffield, England, Stabbed to Death

Karlien Carstens, Okahandja Namibia, Strangled to Death

Felicia Moreno, Hollywood CA, Two Gunshot Wounds

Alejandra Galicio, Bahia Blanca, Argentina, Beaten to Death

Luana Migliarino, Italy, Shot to the Head

The list never ended.

The list never ended.

The list never ended.

I turned away and gripped the railing that led out to the garden.

I hadn't anticipated a gathering to mourn those who'd been *murdered.*

I didn't know them, but I felt lost in the dark.

I took a step outside to smoke before dodging through the crowd to shake hands with the transgender man who spoke and try to make a connection.

He looked up and past me as I walked briskly up to him, putting my hand out to shake his.

"Hi, I'm Sean Mune,"

"Hi Sean,"

"-Thank you so much for…"

My outreached hand hung there awkwardly.

"-the presentation,"

The man who'd been staring off next to Blue seemed to wake up. His eyes snapped to attention as he took Blue's hand and placed it in mine. Blue's eyebrows shot up as he smiled brightly,

"Oh! Sorry, "He chuckled, "I can't see."

"Oh! No problem," I said, apologetic as I squeezed his arm warmly with my other hand.

He was in his late-forties, blind, and transgender? I was in awe.

"Your presentation was very touching, thank you."

"Well thank you." He smiled.

I hung there for a moment. "Can I- Can I ask you a few questions? I really don't know much about Trans people in Fresno, I've been trying for months to find some other people like me,"

I've been dying to ask, I begged inside.

"Sure," He leaned in to hear over the chatter.

I felt like I had gotten an audience with the Dali Lama. I confessed my realization of my being transgender and asked questions on medication, frequency, and resources.

"How did you know?" I asked, "How long ago?"

He told me about being raised in rural Idaho. And never having a name for what he felt. He'd been blind since he was very young and had started transition when he was nearly 40, the average age for transition at that time.

"I really want to meet more transmen," I said excitedly,

Blue elbowed the man next to him, this time startling him from another conversation he'd been having, "BJ! I want you to meet Sean,"

BJ took my hand, a little confused.

"Sean wants to start transition." He explained.

BJ's eyes lit up as he shook my hand a little tighter. I was only the fourth Transman known in the county and a welcome addition to the tiny club.

I made it a point to visit Blue that week, and every few weeks after.

Blue liked to knit by the TV with the right arm of his recliner pressed against the screen. He said he could see the light changes out of the corner of his eye. He liked watching comedy the most and I would hear him burst out into roars of laughter while I'd fix lunch for us. I couldn't wait to hear more stories about him and his ongoing adventures speaking to sexuality and gender classes, to state politicians, and other people of power on Transgender and handicap inclusive services needed in Fresno and the rest of California.

When he wasn't pursuing justice, he was writing his master's thesis in social work on an old computer that utilized a magnifying glass. I remember Blue would crane his head to the side and peer perpendicular at the screen. He sat tapping 5" letters into his documents and guiding the mouse around with precision. God I loved that brilliant man.

"How'd you know you were trans when you were young?" I asked.

"Well, they didn't have a word for it back then," He said, gripping his sandwich. "I just sort of knew I wasn't like my sister. I wanted to be like my dad, and do the things my dad did."

"How did your parents take it?"

"They didn't take it well." He frowned. "They thought I was a tomboy, but they got mad about it as I got older. They forced me to wear dresses. I hate dresses."

I smirked. "How'd you know they didn't look good on you, Blue?"

He chuckled.

"-Cause I'd get dirt on it, every time! My mom would whoop me if I came in the house with a dirty dress on, so I never could play with the other boys." He scowled.

"I would've hated dresses too, Blue." I apologized.

I reflected on his story as we finished lunch in silence, the comedy from the TV still murmuring from the living room. I looked around his grease stained kitchen walls and the piles of dust that had accumulated on the discolored floor. I never thought about how much my cleaning relied on my ability to *see* dirt.

"Do you ever get sad Blue? Like, depressed?"

"Sure I do. Why?"

"I've been alone a lot of my life, but I've never felt so lonely as starting transition by myself. All I've got to share this with is you and BJ. My coworker's been comin' down on me real hard because my voice is changing. They're making fun of me, and when I tell them not to, they pretend like I'm the one with the problem."

Blue scoffed in disgust.

"I love my job, but I don't know what to do. I feel lonely, and it's making me sad… and now I'm feeling sad all the time." I covered my face with my hands.

"Comedy." He answered.

"Really?"

"-Yep. When I get depressed or I'm feeling real low, I turn the TV on to the comedy channel and leave it on, day and night, until I can laugh about it again."

"How long does that take?"

"Not that long."

"*How* long?"

"Just leave it on 'til you're not sad anymore."

I went home and took his advice. I turned on comedy when I was feeling sad, for as long as I was feeling sad, until I didn't feel sad anymore.

The man was a genius.

He helped me to see myself in a whole new way. I was not a gender *fraud* or just some short fat guy with boobs. Blue saw me as a voice. And deep within that voice was a man pushing to be *free*.

And I was a man from the inside out. He recognized my voice from the moment we met to well after testosterone had saddled it into a husky low.

To him, I never changed at all.

I was always that same guy he'd shared the light with one night in a darkened courtyard.

And he was the first person who ever looked close enough to see me for who I truly was;

And then got me to laugh about it.

REST IN PEACE,
BLUE ELIJAH RIGGS
The Transfather of Fresno, California.
A Father to Us All.
MAY 31, 2014

WRONG BODY RIGHT BODY

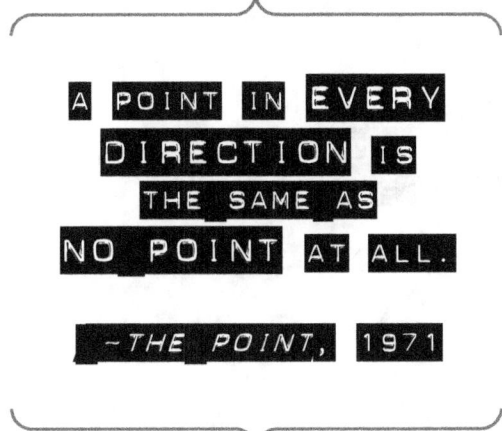

A POINT IN EVERY
DIRECTION IS
THE SAME AS
NO POINT AT ALL.

~THE POINT, 1971

Too many Trans have killed themselves believing they are stuck in the "wrong body." This is insane! We don't kill our best friend because they *ain't right*. Our bodies are our greatest allies and we don't destroy them just because they *ain't all there*.

The point of having a body is to express the meaningfulness that one is to one's self. The point of having no attachments to that body is to peaceably move through accusations of what we "should be", yet *aren't*. The foremost accusation Transpeople face is their 'being in the wrong body'.

But, for there to be a 'wrong' body, there must be a 'right' body. Problem is, there *is no right body*. There is just *your* body. You aren't merely occupying a part of the body, you *are* the body. And it's the only one you get. Believing the body is a separate thing from us is a false argument: A fight with a unicorn. The body is *not* a cage to hold us in. This idea of 'right body, wrong body' has driven many to commit suicide, which was its design.

Believing that you are *stuck* in the wrong body is a mistake of not understanding what you *are*. It makes suicide seem logical: To destroy one's cage to be free. But this idea is actually perpetuated by our abusers, who insist we "cannot escape" our body's sex or gender. They say this to impose their own cage on us, a cage of the mind.

But we believe we are the seed which houses our own inner creator. We have the right to hatch our own inner Buddha, our Soul's expression, or our Christ through *possessing* and altering our state of being, rather than destroying it. We are swirling little universes. And who was ever meant to stay a seed forever? Madness! There is nothing *wrong* with owning and designing your own custom body. It is obvious how this toxic argument on body 'rightness' was started. During a time when we had no words to express our existence, we were limited in our *visibility*. With only a few meaningful ways to express our Selves, we hoped to be barely understood.

And as every human does, we hoped we weren't alone in our suffering. But now, our language around *being* abounds and our connections with each other flourish. It's time to put this harmful and hate filled concept of 'right body' 'wrong body' to rest, so that we may finally end this type of suffering.

As a transgender person, much of my own suffering comes from others *perceiving* me as separate from my own body, as if "I" were merely goods to be *sampled*. My body, now seen as a possession of "I", is then ready to be stolen, destroyed, and trespassed upon. In public, people claim the right to momentary or partial ownership of me by soliciting my attention and time without consent, and without ceasing.

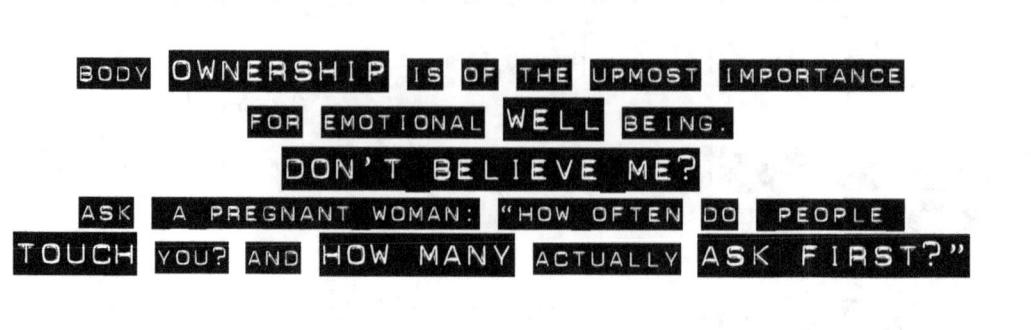

BODY OWNERSHIP IS OF THE UPMOST IMPORTANCE FOR EMOTIONAL WELL BEING. DON'T BELIEVE ME? ASK A PREGNANT WOMAN: "HOW OFTEN DO PEOPLE TOUCH YOU? AND HOW MANY ACTUALLY ASK FIRST?"

When one makes the body synonymous with "occupation of property", the violation of one's property feels naturally and emotionally unattached.

And when you feel lawfully gendered by way of your *sex* (i.e. male = man) you will faithfully solicit the myth that people feel an inherent urge to 'act' manly or womanly. Upon seeing *my* body, a 'vehicle' which must appear to be in a gendered tail spin, many people have clamored to take the wheel of my 'possession', questioning my very right to have a say in it *at all*.

People like parents, friends, teachers, religious figures, lovers, bosses, psychologists, doctors, and common bystanders.

You can tell them all day long that they're wrong, but they won't hear you. Fear is a deafening noise. Instead, thank them for their observation and confess that (whatever their complaint) is what makes you *happy*. Their anxious accusations can subside with a simple confession of *faith in yourself*, especially when the evidence is your happiness, of which there is of course, no cure.

And, if you find you are *not* happy, tell them you have not found your happiness yet, and ask them not to spoil it for you. This does not mean you'll never be happy. We all go through deserts of dissatisfaction, but nothing in life is without ebb and flow. *Your job is to get in the flow.*

Society's alarming need to "fix" our identity is deeply seated in our TV culture. Commercialism brags of how its products can do something to *right* our bodies. This lies with the assumption that we must change to become something *wanted*. I can't watch the TV without someone screaming, "Mmm! Satisfying!"

The crux of every commercial is the assumption we are all burned out on who we are *being*. Something must be fundamentally flawed or *wrong* with us that must be fixed *right now*. The structure of western thought is unhinged by the person who *owns* and *admires* themselves and feels the need for next to *nothing*. In fact, I would say that people have been conditioned to hate and fear those who are content with their poverty, and those who have no drive to chase riches and the myth of 'success'. This is to say, they feel no urge to trade their precious time for money and possessions. Imagine what *being* content within my body means, and more importantly, how it clarifies what I *really need*. Can you imagine rebelling against this consumer's pit by *loving* our Selves as an act of rebellion? And treasuring being a precious nobody so much that it seems ridiculous to *force* beauty products, laser hair removal, paying for programs to control our own weight, taking jobs that we hate, or abusing substance to avoid our Selves?

Were we to set *our own damn standards* on "rightness" by giving way to self acceptance as a jovial FREE FOR ALL, the western world would be a distant memory! A wholly satisfying breakup to an otherwise abusive relationship!

Tell your TV to stop trying to fix you and turn the damned thing off.

Right now you possess the language to create whatever identity you *want*, whether empowered or helpless. Identity is nothing if not a fictitious narrative that needs *no* evidence to hold true!

Our culture is obsessed with *realness* and originality.

What most don't seem to connect is: this is why we are plagued with feelings of loneliness.

The truth is: At our best, we are unoriginal. At our worst, we are *unimaginative*.

This is something to celebrate! It means we aren't the only one! We aren't *alone.* The point of Identity is to become a delight to one's self. That's *it*. Originality is a myth. The universe turns on itself like a kaleidoscope. What is *being* is being all over the place and will eventually come round again. Don't fret. It means you are not a separate part, but a glimpse of the whole. Even if you are not seeing it right now.

In this way, the universe has insured that we are *never* alone.

ORIGINALITY IS UNNATURAL.

My own dysphoria comes from the limitations I feel in owning and designing my own sex's self definition. My body was dust and came together to frame this art and someday, it will be dust again, just as it is within this kaleidoscope universe. But, to say that I have no right to *redesign* myself as I see fit is a miscarriage of my basic right to pursue happiness.

My physical sex came into this world with *no* instructions on how to use it. While others seemed to be masterfully tuned into their sex (which seemed to dictate their identity and suggest their abilities) my genitals seemed disappointingly devoid of any such voice of destiny; Remaining silent as an unplugged radio.

This body does not tell me who "I" is anymore than my belly button talks to me.

I've come to realize that "I" and my body is just meant for *me*. I can love it or I can hate it, but it is mine to do with as I please. As much as some would like me to put my ear to my genitals like I was listening to the Oracle at Delphi, my genitals don't talk to me.

It really doesn't say anything about me at all.

THEREFORE, MY POTENTIAL IS LIMITLESS.

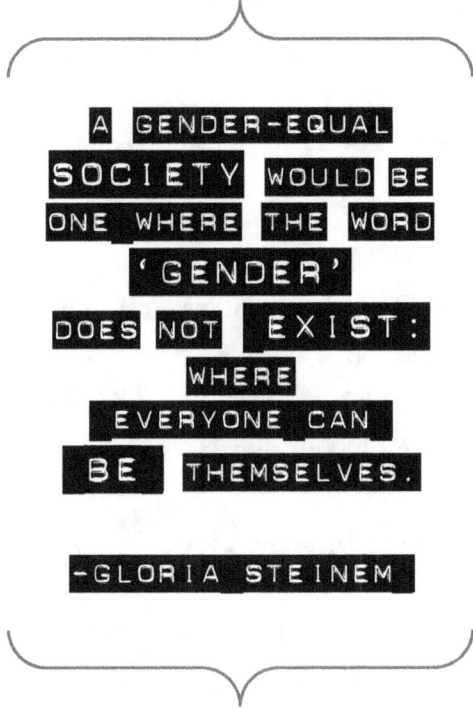

A GENDER-EQUAL SOCIETY WOULD BE ONE WHERE THE WORD 'GENDER' DOES NOT EXIST: WHERE EVERYONE CAN BE THEMSELVES.

-GLORIA STEINEM

Inequality pervades our language like cockroaches in the rot. The connection between our being seen and our being treated as unequal go hand in hand. This is due to our flawed language. Outside the identities and roles our everyday words afford us, there's a strange sort of silence. Larger-than-life identities are near inexpressible, as people who occupy the "in-between" spaces remain both *unseen* and undefined. The Agobi naturally occupy these magical in-between places. People cannot cross over two planes of *being* without someone opening wide the gates, and we are its gatekeepers. Agobis use the invisibility of this "unnamed" in-between space to our advantage. We are able to give people who love us access to new ways of *being*, and effectively deter others who only seek to imprison us with their (accusatory) definitions. Agobis naturally defy definition in order to create abundant creative space in which to thrive. As we pledge to boxes of identity, we lose bits of the flexibility we need to open wide the gate for others to *flow* free. We also inevitably meet the resistance of people's condemnation and disbelief the moment we begin to grow again.

In contrast, the Agobi who flows freely remains magically blameless: For what is there to condemn or resist in someone whom *you don't know* you don't know? As multidimensional beings, we sometimes find connecting with others difficult simply because we don't always exist within our language and so remain *unknowable*. We are most often only understood with either obscene one dimensional indications to our sex like "He," or "She," or the more dehumanizing term like "It". Let me give you an instance of what that looked like in my life. Before 2004, I had no idea what a female-to-male transsexual (FtM) was. It did not exist *to me*. If an FtM had walked up to me and shook my hand, I would not have *seen* them. I would've seen a man, or a woman. Regardless of their appearance and regardless of what they said, I lacked the language for this to exist.

When I began to define the deeper parts of my identity in 2005-2006 and chose to align with a more male profile, some people mistook my journey as a "transition" they'd heard of.

And to some, I am *she*. To others, I am *he*. I now use this magic to *flow* through the in-between spaces.

The truth is, neither are *right*. They only reflect what they see and what they want me to see too. After all, we assume a person's identity only by what we know, regardless of fact. Neither way is *important* or has any value of itself. If I want to be seen, I must use *language*. As an Agobi (i.e. a-go-between), I must create a fresh language around *being* in order to thrive.

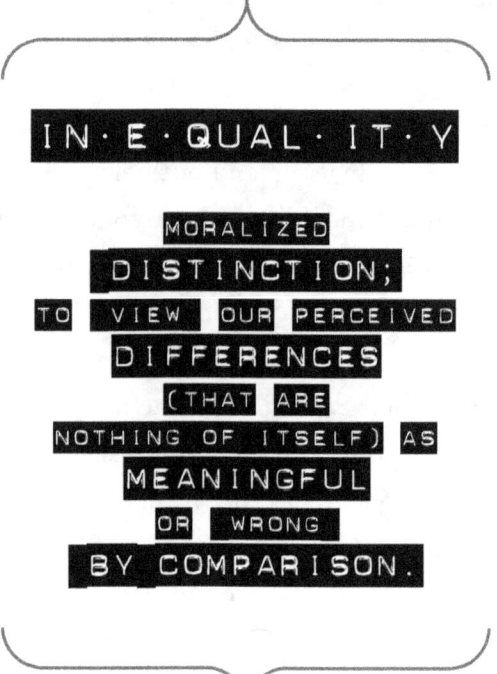

IN·E·QUAL·IT·Y

MORALIZED DISTINCTION; TO VIEW OUR PERCEIVED DIFFERENCES (THAT ARE NOTHING OF ITSELF) AS MEANINGFUL OR WRONG BY COMPARISON.

When you exist outside of what is perceived, you're going to get odd reactions that don't align with your self-perception. Even after creating your identity to someone, their reactions greatly depend on the development and maturity of their *own* identity.

This also means: How people perceive you *still* has nothing to do with you.

———————————

"I have a grandson like that," A grandmother once told me, "He like to wear dresses too."

I stared. It was a cold winter. I dressed in thick heavy black jeans, a camouflage shirt, and hadn't shaved in a week. *Too?* I thought, confused.

"Do you grow breasts when you take hormones?" she asked.

I was shocked, but entertained, and smirked. My head was shaved in a mohawk and I still had triple D breasts in a sling against my chest, awaiting removal. *Clearly* my existence had never occurred to her. She thought I was *already* male on my way to being female. *How cute.* I didn't know whether or not to be flattered by her attempt to relate, but I couldn't be mad that this Betty White had genuinely reached out to *know* me.

"No, no," I laughed, "I've already been there, done that."

She stared, *confused.*

"I was raised a *girl*," I smiled. "Now I'm heading in another direction,"

I watched her stop a moment and stare blankly as this new universe that was "I" burst into her consciousness with an inaudible pop. Several moments passed before she came to.

"Well!" she exclaimed, shifting in her chair.

I'd awakened her from the matrix and she saw me, perhaps, for the first time.

I had made magic! This new in-between space was *real.* And in that moment, I had given up something precious to gain an ally.

I gave up *untouchable anonymity.* I had been alien to her: a house with no windows. But by bursting into her consciousness I had become *visible,* giving us the potential for only either true human *connection*… or a vicious confrontation of the reality that *I exist.*

I learned early on to clarify my gender identity *only* with those I could benefit from knowing me and those I would not be devastated to lose. No one needs clarification, but I offer my Self to stay connected with this world, in hopes that I can bridge the gap for others to be visible without worry.

I understand how identity works: If my dad calls me a big old unicorn it does not steal away any more of my identity than if he were to call me a big old girl-boy. I am just as *invisible* to him as ever.

My identity is quite safe, even if he *knows what I know about 'me'*, because he is powerless to change it at all *without* my cooperation.

Sometimes I imagine how we could efficiently expand our language to include *shamanic shape shifters* like myself. What if a group of interstellar beings visited us who did not possess our binary sex? How else could we honor a species that hasn't a distinct genital profile? Or ones whose sex organs cycled with the seasons? We would have to adapt our language to either include or dehumanize them. Most would, at least initially, resort to our standard aggressive gender expressions: "He", "She", "It". People, please.

It's time. It's time to expand our language to include the whole human experience.

To grow our consciousness, we must grow our potential with a language that has the depth to animate our identity to others in a way that does not render us *undesirable/disposable* in comparison. Most importantly: we must not deduce what we see in others, or else we will treat people as inferior simply because think, *"We know what 'them' is."*

TO RESIST SOMETHING, IT MUST FIRST EXIST. OTHERWISE WE ARE JUST RESISTING OUR SELF, PRETENDING IT IS SOMETHING ELSE.

GENDER & ORIENTATION

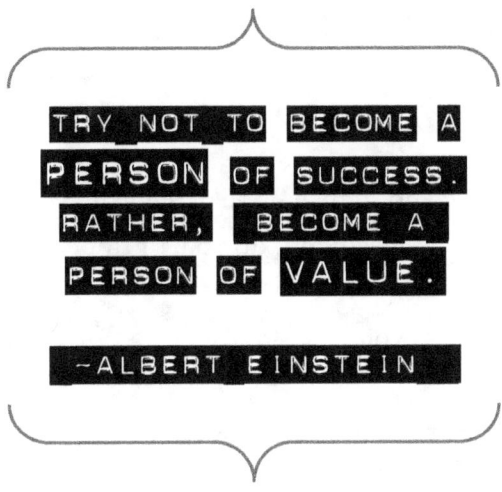

TRY NOT TO BECOME A **PERSON** OF SUCCESS. RATHER, BECOME A PERSON OF **VALUE**.

-ALBERT EINSTEIN

I'm sitting on a wooden stool at the end of a lesbian bar with my hoodie up to my chin. I'm far enough away that I don't catch sight of faces who only assume by my hairy face and plaid coat that I'm just a penis looking for three-way with their girlfriend.

As if! The thought of crawling into bed with some of these girls would make even the most liberal part of me want to stick a bag over my *own* head.

Not my cup o' tea, thank you.

This skirt n' boot wearing goddess who asked me here tonight rubbed elbows with me whenever she glanced a couple staring, and laughed whenever I smiled back at them, cross eyed.

A lesbian had walked right up to yell at me not long ago. Something about me not belonging here. She sounded like my presence was an assault on *her* sex. But yelling at me because my pussy looks like the three billy goats gruff made about as much sense as setting my chair on fire because I looked like I enjoy arson.

Okay, it's on.

So I lost my shirt and displayed my chest scar. "Clearly my sex *isn't* a weapon," I said.

To which the girl skulked down the bar a few more chairs.

Tonight though, I asked this goddess sitting next to me if I could take her on a real date.

"You're trans and I like you, but I'm a lesbian…"

"Okay, (I can see that.)"

Followed by several minutes of silent hand holding.

She piped up, "…But I like you… and you're a transguy. I don't know. What does that make me?"

"You seem to think you know an awful lot about me, I mean, 'Trans, transguy, *not* a lesbian, a guy…? How are you so sure of *me* while so confused about *yourself*?" I teased.

"*I'm* a Lesbian." She stated flatly.

"Okay (I can see that). So what is it about me that makes you *un*-lesbian?" I asked.

"I don't know. I mean I *shouldn't* like you,"

"---Yea, that sounds like some pretty powerful magical Unicorn shit." I laughed,

"Don't laugh!" She pinching me, giggling, "I don't know what you mean."

"Well, outside of *this-*" I said, circling my face, "How do you *want* to be seen?"

"As a Lesbian."

I gave a quick *swish* and *flick,* "Poof! You're a Lesbian!"

She chuckled again. I stared into her eyes. I could see she felt the magic in my possibility, but she couldn't quite shake her self-addressed label.

I know how it feels to have the threat of someone taking away your identity in a single sentence; I wanted her to be free to be whatever she truly *wanted* and eat her cake too. I want her to see the freedom in that wild undiscovered country of a Love without labels.

"I would still love to take you on a date *as* a Lesbian," I added.

"I can't. You know I can't." She stared at the bar.

"For serious? why." I took her hand and frowned.

"Because you're a *man*." I scowled at the label, "-you have a male appearance." She defended.

"There you go with the name calling again. You really have no idea *what* I am, do you," I tipped her chin up to face me.

"I don't want to be perceived as a straight woman when I'm next to you,"

I pursed my lips thoughtfully,

 "Let me show you something." I scooted down three stools and spoke over the crowd.

"What are you?"

She seemed confused.

"What are you right now? Gay? Straight?"

"-Lesbian."

"-Lesbian!" I cheered and scooted closer until one stool was between us.

"What are you now?"

"You don't get it." She said sadly into her drink, flustered.

"Oh I *get* it." I said reassuringly, scooting in to put my arm around her. "Can I ask you something?" She nodded lowly.

"Say I had a goldfish. And I let you take that goldfish home so you could love that fish and live happily together. Would people see you as a greater gold star lesbian because you took a goldfish home rather than me?"

"Are you intentionally confusing me, *sir*?" she gave me a suspicious look.

"No! I'm using cyclical logic to highlight a ridiculous principle. My being *whatever I am* does not make you any *less* of *whatever you want to be* than if you decided to love a goldfish instead of me." She hesitated. I had circled the great misnomer of the Gay/Straight alienation. Somewhere inside her, she *did* love me, but her friends did not love her love of me. Ironic how a community defined by sexual freedom in identity would exile the ones who pioneer it *further*.

"We don't have to go out." I reassured her, "I just want you to be *free* to love whomever you wish on your own terms. Isn't *this* why we identify as queer?"

The light came on in her eyes.

She looked up, took a hold of my beard, and gave me a big kiss on the cheek. But I knew: My world, as vast as it was, frightened her. She needed support (i.e. permission) from those who angrily opposed her freedom to love what *they* did not understand. Truth was, her attraction to my transness shamed her, and I was so embracing of her expression of that shame, that she felt a loss to define the *real* problem.

You probably assume the problem is "society" or her "not being accepting", or that it truly was against her nature to love or be attracted to me, but that was not it. *Not at all.*

There is a fundamental flaw in the human emotion that *asks for permission*. What are we so afraid of? We all die, and in dying, become dust. And the dust is the truth of us: Being neither male nor female, married nor straight. Not rich. Not in a hurry. Not violent. Not envious. But a wonderer, far and wide.

We defined sexual orientation in order to help us find each other, not to disregard our *own* feelings and experiences of attraction. Identity is manufactured, therefore, treating orientation as a fixed universal law is unnatural. The problem in making your attractions *wrong* is that you're forced to *erase yourself* in order to comply with orientation over attraction.

What is the point in asking, "Who am I attracted to *other than* what I already decided is *wrong?*" What a miserable oversight!

Identities, including sexual orientation, is *not* wrong. It simply isn't fixed because *identity isn't concrete.* Identity is nothing other than what "I" make of it or am compelled to be. I've met more than a few boring souls whose entire existence was made to avoid their attractions, while simultaneously policing everyone else's. How miserable to exist in your own *absence*!

Struggling with one's orientation is as bizarre as suiting up to go fight the Unicorns. Instead of beating ourselves up because we don't understand our attractions, a better question would be: Does this identity *work*? In other words, does this attraction bring meaning which enhances, strengthens, and motivates me? Or does it make me feel tired, unmotivated, and *not* at peace?

If you could pull back the curtain on all the suffering you endure in discovering who "I" is, you'd see that you only suffer in moments when you either *resist* your truth or when you allow others to be heralds of *your* sexual identity.

It's painful to be *unseen,* but it's even more painful to *not allow yourself to exist at all.*

Not everyone is gifted with eyes for the goldfish in the room, but those who do need *special* acceptance and support from their friends. Goldfish are easy to love. It's finding someone with the strength of character to *acknowledge their feelings* that seem to be overwhelmingly absent in the room.

Let your friends know: If they fall in love with someone *completely opposite* of what you imagined, you'd still love and respect them, and they'll still have you as their ally.

Because someday, if you're lucky, someone might just stand up for you because *you* are the goldfish.

EAT MY CRACKERS

My friends and I play this game where we name our "gay exception": that is, that super hot movie star that does not fit our assumed orientation, but we would jump at a chance to sleep with despite their physical sex. This works well with gay men too. Just say "Young Eliza". If they're not *too* young, they'll go along with it.

Mine? Well, Hugh Jackman. I mean, from *Wolverine* to *Jean Val Jean*? That man, in tight jeans, could eat my crackers in bed *any* day. And for all you nay sayers who absolutely are repulsed by sex outside your 'orientation', lemme ask you this:

Who is that one famous person (pop star, author, revolutionary) of the 'correct' sex that you would *appropriately* jump at the chance to snuggle in bed with??

Think about that a moment.

If they were *exactly* as you imagined: charming and seductive and sexy; and they invited you to their house… Would you go?

Hell Yes.

But let's say the minute you accept, they tell you that despite your obvious attraction to each other, *they* were born with confusing genitals: a clit that was 6" too long or a dick that was 6" too short.

Would it mean that you were *never* attracted to them in the first place? No!

Would you *reconsider* your 'orientation' to be intimate with someone you admire this much??

Hell yes!

You might lie about it in the morning, but you'd want them right there and then! This is because you don't *actually* hate dick or pussy. In that moment you'd hate what you've made it *mean.*

"DOES THIS MAKE ME GAY OR STRAIGHT?"

This is the #1 question I've gotten with someone *newly* attracted to me.

What do I tell them?

"No darlin', all it means is I *rock* your world."

Does that make you bisexual? *Absolutely not.*

Does it mean you are still attracted to someone who might also happen to have genitals that confuse you? *Sure.*

Does that make it wrong? No! That's ridiculous.

Not every sexual encounter you'll have with someone trans will be awesome, but let's be fair. Not every sexual encounter you'll have with just *anyone* will be awesome either.

That isn't because trans is bad. You just didn't enjoy that *one* person's flavor. So why do people who've *never* been with someone trans seem to set the highest standards of what is acceptably beautiful in a transperson? Hypermasculinizing or Hyperfeminizing someone in order to deem them acceptably attractive hurts *all of us.*

Because my physical sex and gender serve as a paradox of contradictions, I often see the doubt on people's faces who are devoted to perpetuating their myth of orientation.

The denial of our attraction because my genitals don't fit your imagination really is... just childish and *unhealthy*.

Going between these gendered worlds has given me a certain advantage of observing people. As I have no internal conflict over my own identity, I'm able to be just about anything to anyone, without compromising my Self at any time. With this tool of adaptation, I have had the privilege of enjoying many personally edifying love lives with those I've admired. I've experienced love with a straight woman, with a gay man, with a gay transman, a bi man, a straight man, a bi woman, a straight transman, a gay male couple, a dedicated butch lesbian, and a queer androgynous person.

What does that make *me*?

ABUNDANTLY LOVED.

What do we all share in common when it comes to Love? *Mutual admiration and respect.*

That is true love. True love honors *whatever* body we have today, whatever choices we make, and whatever persona we use to celebrate our *being alive*.

You can't love someone you don't admire, but you can admire someone without being in love with them. It's when attraction aligns with admiration (regardless of the physical sex of either person) that sparks fly. 95 times out of 100, you fall for someone *before* you've even seen what's below their naval. So why is that so horrifying for some to admit when they fall for someone who has unexpected genitals?

Admittedly, I don't feel admiration for many male men except on rare occasion. Not because of their body but because of what I hear come from between their ears. And of those men, I'm even more rarely attracted to their body. But of those few I admire *and* am attracted to, they are usually unavailable, unattracted to, or unadmiring of me. Does my attraction for persons with genitals that don't resemble mine mean that I'm straight?

Hell no.

It means I know what I want in a person, and finding them doesn't consist of me *qualifying* their genitals. I find women much easier to admire, find attractive, and sometimes, more readily open and available. For example, I very much crush on butch lesbians because, as a general rule, I admire their values and I am attracted to the strength they've had to develop to survive. My own life has echoed many of these feelings and qualities, a trait that I can easily fall in love with.

I also love gay men. Specifically, bears. Why? Partly because I like the way they *relate* to me and I generally like their attitudes on community and life. My attraction has nothing to do with *straight* feelings. The fact remains, I enjoy queer sex, especially with another masculine person. I enjoy strong, empathetic, masculine, hairy people who maintain healthy relationships outside of the bedroom, regardless of their physical sex.

In love there's no top/bottom. There is no hierarchy. We don't strip mine the one's we love by taking what we want and leaving the rest in a heap of rubble. That's extortion, not admiration. Love provides a safe space for our lover to share their innermost self with us, to fall apart, and rebuild their most vulnerable parts back up.

It's unfortunate that amidst the thrills marriage equality promises, that the myth of fixed orientation still pervades. We may find hairy people harder to admire. This doesn't mean we wouldn't hop into bed with a hairy person whom we are heads over heels with. Orientation is not an indisputable fact like our eye color. When we discover something we dislike with someone we're *wild for*, at this point we're merely negotiating *preference*. If my lover didn't like being penetrated, I would be sad, but I wouldn't *lie* and say I'd never date "their type".

My attraction doesn't change when I meet a very attractive person and a nosey friend tells me they have genitals that are *different* than they'd expect.

Now, does your preferences change? *Yes.* Because preference is an interpretation of qualities that another person has. If someone changed how I interpreted it, it changes my preference.

For example: If the smell of deodorant reminds me of when my dad came home after his shift and gave me a great big hug before bed, I might prefer men who wore deodorant and shaved.

Now let's say I dated someone who wears lots of deodorant and shaves. They also pretended they liked me before they stole my money and blamed me when I broke it off. Suddenly, deodorant reminds me of betrayal.

Then I run into a Yogi master who grows soft hairs on his chin. He is very kind and patient with me and invites me to spend time with him. He doesn't use any chemicals on his body, but wears clean garments. When I hug him, he smells sweet and warm. My memory of him makes me smile.

I now have a preference for men who do *not* wear deodorant and do *not* shave.

See my point?

We like what we like because of the stories we experience explaining *why*.

Why we prefer what we prefer, and why who we love *can* change over time with each new emotional experience.

All while we pretend we were always this way, when we simply *weren't*.

GENDER AS A REFLECTION

WHEN SOMEONE SHOWS YOU WHO THEY ARE BELIEVE THEM; THE FIRST TIME.

-MAYA ANGELOU

I stood at the car shop counter. A trail of people swayed drearily behind me. The cashier took my ticket, glanced at me a moment too long, and rung me up.

Okay, so I looked androgynous. I'd been taking hormones for 3-4 months now, my name was androgynous, my height, my weight, my clothes.

I had no gender 'marker' to speak of.

The mechanic slid through the oily door leading to the pit and dropped my keys on the counter, glancing at the paperwork and back at me. "His car's ready." He said briskly before heading out. I stared at my keys as I felt the cashier narrow her eyes, "I'll ring- *her*- out."

The mechanic gripped the doorknob and froze. His head silently wagged.

I realized I'd started something between them.

I glued my eyes on my keys, my heart in my throat.

What do I do now?

He turned on his heel and glanced back at me and then the crowd, who seemed to be waking up. His bristles shaded his expression. "I'll check- *hiiim*- on this register. Over here- *sir*." he flagged me towards the second register, like a dutiful valet.

I looked up nervously. The first cashier put her fists on her hips and seethed.

"I've already rung- *her*- up!"

They paused and turned to me, waiting for my call like a referee in a boxing ring.

I pocketed my keys quickly so I could look up.

The crowd was quiet.

I was uncomfortably aware of the tension I'd generated by the question being asked of me.

What are you?

I threw my hands up half heartedly, half nervous as hell.

"Hey, I don't really *care*! I just want to go *home*." I dropped my money on the counter and slid out the exit without a sound. The crowd froze, deflated by the plug I'd pulled. It frightened me how serious the moment had become.

It took me a long time to understand how gender had occurred that day and what it meant for me. Now I realize: People are *hungry* for connection. Women want to feel understood by other women. Men want to feel included by other men. We affirm our sex's gender like two football fans giving high fives at the stadium, even if we are perfect strangers. This gender game gives us connection and assurance that we are *not alone* in how we feel.

When you assume someone's gender, you'll project your beliefs on how that person wants to be treated. For example, if "Bob", who identifies as a 'man', is attached to behaviors which *he* believes give meaning to his identity as a man (i.e. not crying, lifting heavy objects, being punished for 'acting' female), Bob will also expect that from people he perceives are also *men*. If "Bob" runs into a 'man' named "Jamie" who likes to wear necklaces, grow his hair long, and cried openly when his wife gave him symphony tickets, Bob may project his own feelings of discomfort onto Jamie as if Bob himself had done these *offensive* things.

For example: Bob may feel embarrassed for Jamie. This fear may even make him avoid Jamie in the future. Or, he may look down on Jamie, feeling he is not a 'real man'.

Bob may write him off as a 'fake' man, calling him effeminate names to try and dissuade Jamie from *being* himself.

Bob may feel Jamie is an affront to the idea of 'men' all together and openly persecute him.

Or, Bob may feel sorry for Jamie, believing that he needs a father figure (i.e. a 'real man' with "Bob" attachments). In this scenario, Bob is at a loss for how Jamie can be a 'real man' while behaving in ways that are *not* "Bob" like. This is because:

BOB CAN'T SEE JAMIE.

Bob can only see how Jamie should be more like Bob (and is mysteriously *not*). This desire for *likeness* is instinctual, but it is also *completely* unrelated to reality. Most people become angry at Bob for seeing Jamie as the problem. If instead, Jamie approached Bob, not with anger at his inconvenient behavior, but with a genuine appreciation for Bob's attempts to relate to him, then Jamie can actually set him *free*.

If Jamie realizes that Bob is *Bob's problem,* and by allowing Bob to be Bob and celebrating those differences they have, Jamie can allow Bob time to see that Jamie really likes doing "Jamie" things and it doesn't steal away from Bob doing "Bob" things. Given time to adjust, Bob could start to see how they are both *still* men who can peacefully appreciate each other while being *completely* different.

Bob's obsession with Jamie's identity is overreaching. It would be more appropriate if Bob realized he doesn't understand Jamie at all, and simply *asked*. Unfortunately, most people have real difficulty admitting they don't understand a situation. It often unnerves us to realize something exists outside of what we know. It's a natural function of the lower brain to freak out when something unfamiliar or unpredictable is occurring; it's what's protected us from being eaten by new predators. The most dangerous predators we now see today are the ones that stand on their two feet.

It's presumptive to think Jamie identifies as anything at all. The fact remains: It is irrelevant how Jamie identifies. It's just as inappropriate for Bob to pressure Jamie in this way as in the case that Jamie were female.

Why is it not obvious that Bob is *just* as unhealthy for Jamie as it would be if Jamie identified as a woman? What Bob fails to see is that Jamie is *not* a representation of Bob.

Also, as the "Jamie" in someone's life, we too often fail to see that however Bob chooses to act, his actions are the result of a private conversation Bob is having with *himself*, not Jamie's identity or involvement.

In this scenario, Bob is just acting from his (presumptive) privilege rather than a desire to get to *know* Jamie. I don't blame Bob, but if Bob is aggressive and unwilling to suspend his judgments, Jamie should feel free to *refuse* to participate in 'Bob's problem' all together.

I once heard that the punishment for the judgments we make is having to live with it ourselves.

This is too true in this case. If Bob is incapable of seeing Jamie as a valuable person because of the way Jamie identifies, it's only because Bob, for whatever reason, struggles with a part of himself that he sees in Jamie.

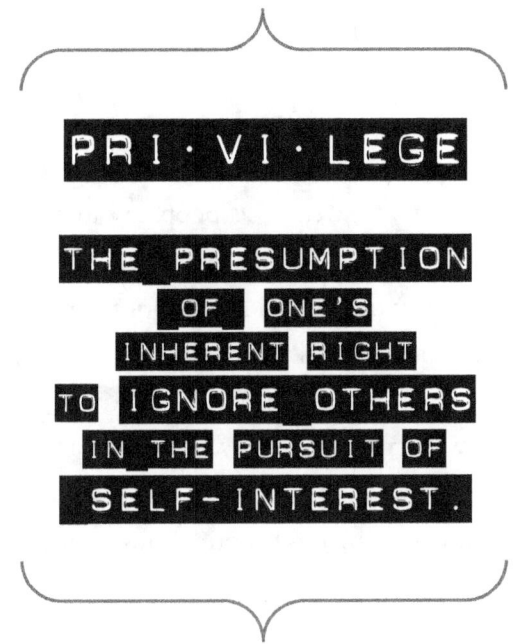

PRI·VI·LEGE

THE PRESUMPTION OF ONE'S INHERENT RIGHT TO IGNORE OTHERS IN THE PURSUIT OF SELF-INTEREST.

That doesn't mean that either Bob or Jamie are bad people. It means that Bob simple can't *see* Jamie's value because Jamie is a wake up call for what Bob doesn't like to see in *himself*. Bob can't see Jamie because Bob keeps getting in the way.

What we all hope is that the "Bobs" in our life would see our behaviors and who we are as a brilliant *new* way of being, and would be himself around us.

We give favor to people of our desirable gender because we wear the same 'jersey'. Yet we don't always favor the gender we identify with. I know many many women who proudly shame and sabotage their own sex. Some also find the freedom of other women disturbing.

Gender is an illusion of what you think you *should* be. When I walked into the car repair shop, the woman didn't see me. She looked at me and saw herself. When I was addressed as 'he', she reacted as if she *herself* had been insulted. Similarly, the man who looked at me saw a resemblance of himself and acted to protect his own projected image. What I realized was: They both identified with me and were confused by their co-worker 'insulting' their sex.

I also realized: A person's objections have *nothing* to do with me. People are very attached to how they see themselves. Whether it be sex, gender, class, or race, people feel a need to police their identity. Secretly, I think we sense that it only takes only *one person* living their own identity to shatter the illusion. And, because my identity entirely bastardizes gender, people regularly rise to the occasion to snuff out, project, fix, or to admonish me on how I should navigate stereotypes because my non-conformity threatens to expose the illusion of *type*.

People will *always* see you as a reflection of who they *could* be.

To one person, I may be a perfect reflection of who they *wish* to be: Someone strong. Someone beautiful. Someone free. They will treat me kindly.

To another, I may be a reflection of the nightmare they fear they *could* be. To be strong. To be beautiful. To be free. They will treat me hideously.

What I realized from all this?

I have absolutely nothing to do with *why* someone treats me poorly. Most aren't even self-aware enough to realize why they are behaving that way either. Confronting the "Bob" in your life is counter-productive, as people who treat others poorly are only actually having a fight with *themselves*. It's best to get out of their way.

Not everyone has to learn about themselves, in fact, some people will die quite happy in the ignorance that is them. And that is okay. Life isn't a rescue mission.

Now, some of you may be angry about Bob's reaction, but I would like to remind you:

How can you object to Bob's intolerance by showing *more* intolerance for Bob?

You can't object without simultaneously validating the argument.

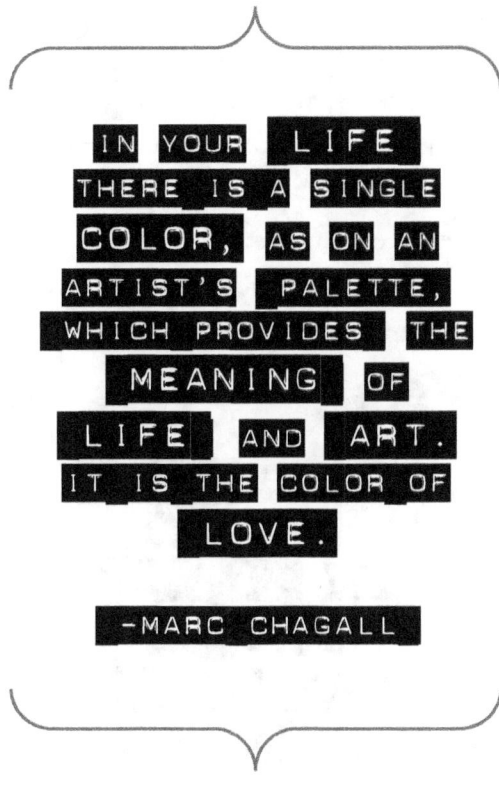

IN YOUR LIFE THERE IS A SINGLE COLOR, AS ON AN ARTIST'S PALETTE, WHICH PROVIDES THE MEANING OF LIFE AND ART. IT IS THE COLOR OF LOVE.

-MARC CHAGALL

The intense fear of Colors.

Colors give meaning to the world around us.

The oranges and yellows sunsets spray over us, giving us quiet longing and hope, while those same colors excite us when they appear as the autumn leaves turn. The wild crystal blue of the arctic ice grant us deep solace, while the shimmering blue of the Florida Keys give us a sense of warmth and playfulness.

Colors give us a sense of meaning. But, when we treat these colors as inherent rather than inventive in it's meaning, the freshness, beauty, and balance we feel with colors are lost.

The 'feminine' in pink is *not* in the pink itself, but in *us*. It's how you interpret the feminine you see in *yourself* that determines whether you are repulsed or attracted to pink. When the color pink covers your body, do you feel elated or fearful? Do you feel belittled or beautiful? Do you feel misunderstood or proud?

What is it in *ourselves* that makes us feel so strongly about the color pink? What is *natural* about rejecting that part of ourselves that feels *pink* too?

Truth is: there is nothing unnatural about color, except how we relate to it. We relate to it as if the colors are a living entity, wearing *us*. Although we admit it is foolish child's play, many adults are still gripped with a real sense of fear, an actual phobia, whenever certain colors or cuts of cloth are applied to their body or attributed to their persona.

Whenever we hesitate to pick up a shirt off the rack because it's color makes us uncomfortable, or we refuse to wear a coat because it's cut suggests we are a different *sex*, we act as color is innately dangerous to who we *really* are.

This fear of colors is worth exploring because it keeps our power eluding us. It keeps us from realizing: who we are does *not* disappear under what we wear.

When I was younger, my mother forbad me from stepping into the clothing section assigned to the 'other gender'. I could physically *see* an invisible line drawn across the aisle. Whenever we walked by, I would brush my hand across the sleeves that edged this foreboding section. A mysterious textile forest of attributes I'd *wished* I'd had and felt sure were buried in the fabric. I was gripped by this inexpressible and shame filled longing to be *brave and strong and secure*.

Whenever I wore clothes for my mother, I felt crushed between the layers of polyester and cotton. I felt weak, vulnerable, belittled, silenced, and restricted.

The laws of my sex wore heavy on my body. Looking back, I only wished someone had given me permission to see clothing and color without the 'scheme'.

The split spectrum of gendered colors kept me feeling burdened and unbalanced.

I'm not saying that I missed the chance to be myself because I didn't have the clothes for it. Clark Kent was Superman long before he got his cape. What I'm saying is: I missed the chance to explore a deeper sense my *being* regardless of the colors I wore. And I missed the opportunity to share myself with the world and by the love and support of my mother.

Now I celebrate the colors with a renewed sense of love and adventure. I understand that colors aren't projections of a *gendered* me. I may wear pink today, but I'm not this fabricated 'story' behind pink (weak, princess, wimpy, timid, overly emotional, eccentric, dramatic)… I'm a person enjoying and sharing a bright color with the world around me.

Pink is whatever *I* wish it to be today. I am not its implied attributes. It is *my* pink.

When people play the game, "My gender color is better than yours", I can laugh right alongside them. It's ridiculous to think that what I wear *affirms* my identity. I have that sense of *being* that has no color at all. I'm not a gender mascot on display; a colorful cartoon illustration of what my sex should look like. I'm one who wears anything I like.

This life was made to display the magic we see inside us.

Try wearing the same color for a month. *Try it.* It will bring up parts of you that you *never* knew existed. You may discover how colors influence your view of your identity. Maybe you've avoided certain colors and clothes you think are *inappropriate* for your sex.

Maybe deep down, you fear the colors expose a vulnerable part of you that *you* haven't come to terms with yet. But I bet it's a part of you that you secretly long to freely *be*.

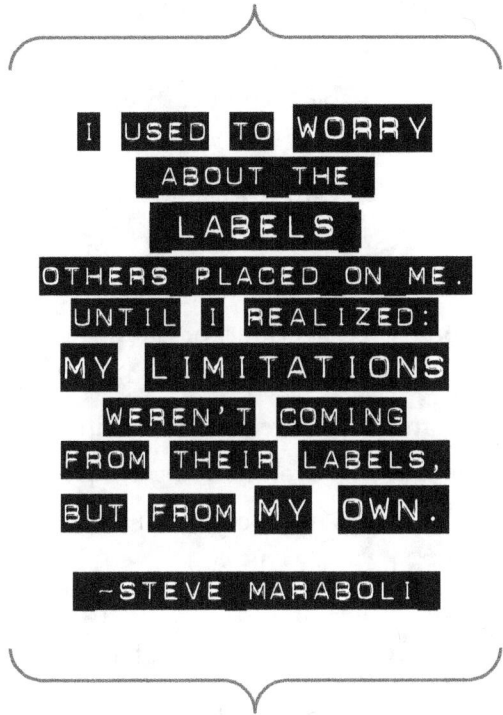

I USED TO WORRY ABOUT THE LABELS OTHERS PLACED ON ME. UNTIL I REALIZED: MY LIMITATIONS WEREN'T COMING FROM THEIR LABELS, BUT FROM MY OWN.

-STEVE MARABOLI

What is the difference between orientation and preference? For starters, preference is our generalized *likes* and *dislikes* we choose arbitrarily. However, when we exaggerate those preferences to *biblical* proportions, we filter our experiences through a mythological story referred to here as "sexual orientation".

Let me give you an example. I can't stand the taste of mint flavored ice cream. *Really.* It feels like I'm eating mouthfuls of icy toothpaste. In fact, I avoid mint toothpaste all together. If there is any other option, I usually take it. I even brush my teeth with mintless strawberry or orange flavors and have faithfully done so for years. My preference against mint (especially in chocolate or toothpaste) is genuine. But to say, "I will *never* enjoy anything mint *ever*, so don't ask," would be an exaggerated, deeply personal *lie*. I confess, I *have* utilized mint in one *odd* fashion. Ever since I was a kid, I assumed gum only came in mint and minty fruit flavors. So, I would dutifully pick out the *mildest* wintermint gum I could find to take on long road trips with me to help pass the time. Now whenever I chew wintermint, I'm filled with this sense of adventure for travel and I crave new exotic destinations! Why? Because I've conditioned my brain to respond positively whenever I add wintermint. In fact, I have on occasion broke open the wintermint gum in planning a trip to reinvigorate my enthusiasm for travel.

My preference (I don't like mint) is *real*.

My preference (I like travelling with wintermint gum) is also *contextual*.

We like or dislike things that hold *meaning* for us. The meaning behind those things *occur* without a legitimate, universal rhyme or reason. One person is spanked and becomes afraid of punishment, while another becomes emotionally attached to the person spanking them.

Each interpretation our brain takes is arbitrary and *meaningless* in comparison. My distaste for mint has absolutely *nothing* to do with whether mint is good or bad, nor acknowledges how mint is useful to the world around me. In this same way, whenever I kiss a person, my brain either goes, "*Yep*", "*Nope*", or "*Yuck*" without reasoning and without acknowledging that person's contribution to my experience.

In this same way, people fall in love all the time *regardless* of either party's physical sex. Fact is, 98% of the time you feel attracted *before* you ever see your crush from the waist down. So, if our orientation is defined as who we are physically attracted, and our attractions occur *regardless* of that persons physical sex, then how is sexual orientation (i.e. attraction based on genitals) *real at all?*

It's not.

Sure, masculinity and femininity have grown up around us and we associate it with... *Whatever*. But to say we are *incapable* of loving someone for a physical feature we *don't* see in everyday life? *That's bullshit and shenanigans!*

Orientation displaces our *feelings* by shoving it through a filter of "acceptable attributes" we require of someone else to even *acknowledge* what we are *already feeling*. How lame!

Some men look just *delicious* in a dress! And to be fair, bald women often turn my head. Who has penises? Who has vaginas? *Who cares!* What does that have to do with what I'm *already feeling?* I'm still attracted to them! In my brain, you might as well say, "Who chews their fingernails? Who's got a manicure?" I don't know! What does *that* matter? That's a pretty useless filter for finding a *great* person. Denying our attractions when they occur outside our norm is simply throwing the baby out with the bathwater. People who don't acknowledge their own attractions are the first to find offense with those who *do*. This is why I believe there is very little language around being attracted to transfolk. Because, to simply say *"I love people"* is to concede to the idea that our attractions are both *arbitrary* (randomly male and/or female) and *contextual* (feminine and/or masculine).

Now, I do believe that people have preferences for partners with an "innie" or an "outie". Partners who shower, or don't. Partners who are round, or tall, or hairless. In this case, we're speaking about contextual *preferences*. So, when we argue over the length of someone's clit instead of their fingernails, *how* is that suddenly referring to our all-powerful orientation?

Rather than just another arbitrary, contextual preference we've built an alter around?

I believe it when someone says they do not find the idea of my genitals attractive. But to say that, out of the whole world, they're not attracted to *anyone* with my set of genitals would be a blatant *exaggeration*. When a person says that they hate penis, what I hear is: you don't prefer the company of people who colonize your space with stereotypical aggressive male (i.e. penis) behaviors. *Me neither!* I find the abuse of privilege the most unattractive trait in *any* person, man or woman; A trait I most often see in people with a penis. However, you can't convince me that if the love of your life woke up and her clit was now 5" too long that you'd sacrifice her on the altar of your infallible orientation. She is still the same woman who makes your heart pump and you *still love her* for who she fundamentally is. After all, her genitals say absolutely *nothing* about her, and to be fair, she probably didn't *sign up for this either.* Just like you, your beloved wants a relationship that honors, cherishes, and shelters their *innermost self.* What good is a lover that constantly judges our outsides and disregards our heart? In the same token, would you instantly stop loving the most cherished man in your life if he had a vulva? *No!* What were you attracted to up until this point?

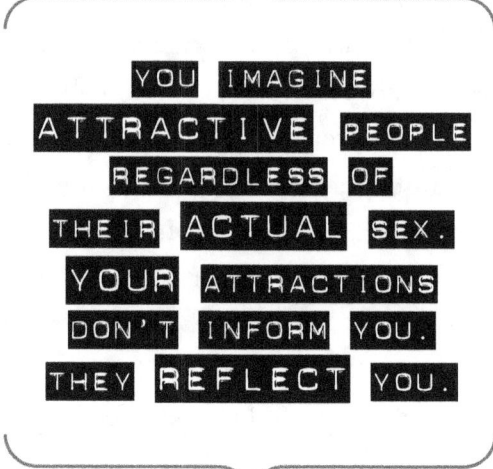

YOU IMAGINE ATTRACTIVE PEOPLE REGARDLESS OF THEIR ACTUAL SEX. YOUR ATTRACTIONS DON'T INFORM YOU. THEY REFLECT YOU.

You *love* because you connected. Deep down, *you didn't fall in love with their skin*, you fell in love with their *persona* and the connection you share together. If the guy is a sleazebag, you wouldn't enjoy him *anyways*, regardless of his tool. And vise versa, you'd *still* be attracted to your girlfriend because *you don't hate dick,* you're afraid of what *you think* dick says about you.

Let's be clear. Whatever you're feeling is your own private conversation. It has absolutely nothing to do with *me* or factual reality. Maybe what you're really terrified of is that being honest with your feelings will lead to you being hurt and that people misunderstand and accuse you of being untrue to a *myth* they assumed all along. *Welcome to my world.* There is no one braver than a person who is honest with *themselves.*

Confessing one's love for a transperson is one of the bravest things I've witnessed because this fearful society demands that it be *authentic.* I don't think anyone actually hates transpeople. As ridiculous as it sounds (because it *is* ridiculous), I believe people have always feared that transfolk have *magic.* Enchantments that expand the boundaries of their horizons beyond anything they thought *possible.* When a cognitive distortion of this magnitude (like sexual orientation) collapses, people don't just realize the earth isn't flat, they feel it *move* under their feet. Trans people are persecuted primarily because our *existence* tells a fundamental truth about our *humanity* that supersedes the mythical stories we tell about ourselves. Meaningful stories *aren't wrong,* they just aren't always *true.*

Truth is: no one understands what you are truly feeling when you fall in love. You just *do.* This is just as true for heterosexuals as it is for everyone else. We just tend to question love and lovers of people who like Trans* and *don't* have the same taste in companionship as we do. Does loving someone transgender betray or change our orientation?

Hell No! Orientation is the story we tell about our preference to make it sound more legitimate. You may discover you prefer someone's flavor that others find very hard to comprehend. That's okay! Ultimately, it doesn't matter what your friends see in your relationship, it only matters what *you see,* because *your* relationship is *not* for them. Loving a person *for who they truly are* is the best gift you can give. Loving someone trans* may just mean that you only like mint if it's on *their* toothbrush!

If you are interested in dating someone transgender, get to know them before you assume they want *anything to do with you.* It's pretty presumptive to start worrying about what sex will be like when you don't even know who we are. Personally, there's a good chance I will have ZERO interest in *you,* other than socially. Assuming every Trans person will automatically want you sexually, especially if your body looks like something between cookie dough and melted ice cream, is pretty presumptive and unattractive of *you.* Many of us have been sexually assaulted by the very people who claimed we just want aimless sex. Transpeople tend to be cautious, as we are too often abused because of what *someone else is feeling.*

Another thing? Don't interrupt someone else's relationship to insert your curiosity... it will not bode well for you, and it will not help you understand yourself better. Sex is *always* awkward the first time, no matter *who* you're with, but it's not any weirder than the first time having sex with *anyone*

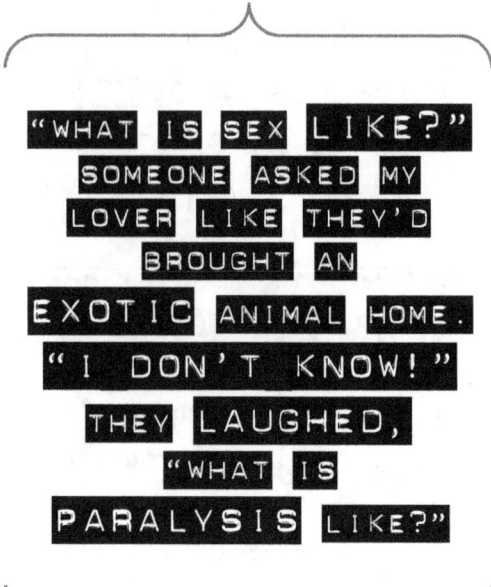

"WHAT IS SEX LIKE?"
SOMEONE ASKED MY
LOVER LIKE THEY'D
BROUGHT AN
EXOTIC ANIMAL HOME.
"I DON'T KNOW!"
THEY LAUGHED,
"WHAT IS
PARALYSIS LIKE?"

else. You just need to *communicate more* to discover what *that* person is interested in. It's not like we have parts from an alien planet, so *relax*! Most people take *getting to know their lover* for granted and assume all body parts have heterotypical preferences i.e. vaginas like penetration and penises like to be touched, but this is *not* true! Not at all! I once had the privilege of meeting a female couple who, in terms of penetration, were exclusively anal! Their reasons were their own, but neither of them had the slightest interest in vaginal play. I found this truly inspiring of two people sitting down and connecting over their *common preference!* In this case, what would sex have to do with their orientation? i.e. the word they use to generalize and describe their sexual preferences?

It's a gift to give pleasure to someone you like. It's even more gratifying to be what they *openly* prefer, which can change over time.

When's the last time you asked your lover what they enjoy?

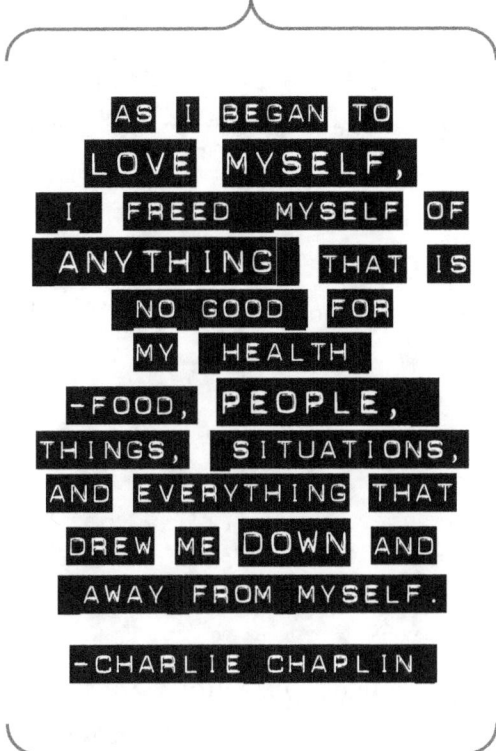

AS I BEGAN TO LOVE MYSELF, I FREED MYSELF OF ANYTHING THAT IS NO GOOD FOR MY HEALTH -FOOD, PEOPLE, THINGS, SITUATIONS, AND EVERYTHING THAT DREW ME DOWN AND AWAY FROM MYSELF.

-CHARLIE CHAPLIN

I'd known Frida for a year and a half. She was a very sweet gramma type lady that everyone proudly called their own. She'd been single now for the past 15yrs and proudly independent. Frida always had this gift of making me feel right at home and welcome in her comfy home. Her house was awash with warm female energy. I loved visiting Frida to chew on shaved ice chips and talk about her dog and about life. Her demeanor was as silky as any domestic goddess. Her passions included visiting sick friends and joining the slow motion interpretive dance group for seniors at her local church. She appealed to every type of person with her soft sing-songy voice, that only sounded brass when someone was being left out. She was a true lover of the underdog and quick with a smile and a hug. Her eyes made it difficult to drive in the dark so I frequently accompanied her to evening events at the theater and escorted her home after. She asked me how my relationship at the time was going and about our families involvement in our lives. "My family doesn't support us being together." I said dryly.

Surprised, she replied, "Oh? Is it because-" And she named off some typical heterosexual reasons why a family would be too conservative to approve of a man and a woman living together.

I had forgotten! She didn't know I was trans!

I'd just stepped in a conversation where I'd have to explain my identity. Suddenly my head was whirring with the most likely outcomes of this revelation.

"Noooooo…" I trailed off, "It's not because of religion or anything…"

I stopped, hoping that would be it.

She waited silently with her hands in her lap looking at me until the air in my lungs began to stale.

Man oh man. Tell her?

Don't Tell Her.

Tell her?

Don't Tell her?

I sucked in all the brave air I could and blurted,

"They're against me being with her because I…"

How do I describe this? Another pause. Another breath.

"I'm female. Our families think it's *wrong* because I used to be a girl."

The car hummed as we slid down the dark street.

"You what? You used to be a *girl?*" She said curiously in her still sing-songy voice. I could feel my face flush.

"Yes." I held my breath. It was too hard to see her face in the dark.

Damn this nighttime. I didn't give her a way out of this situation. I should have waited.

"-You mean you didn't *tell* me? This whole time!" I heard her grin with each bouncing syllable. Surprised, my heart burst with gratitude, relieved I hadn't lost my best friend in the trenches of this sudden gender bend.

"Well, I didn't *think* about it until just now!"

"-What!"

"Yeah! I realized you didn't understand why my family would be weird about her and I, and then I realized it's because you didn't know I was queer,"

"-But you're straight right?"

"*Noooooo*. Not really. We're pretty queer."

"-But you're a man, right?"

"Noooooooo-" I clenched my jaw. "I didn't really transition to 'become a man'. I transitioned to become *me*." She contemplated that a moment as we turned into her driveway.

"I like that." She smiled. "It makes *sense*."

She held the door handle a moment longer and stared off at the porch light, "I'm surprised I've never heard it explained that way before... It makes perfect sense. Well," She continued, patting my knee, "*I* like you." I leaned over and gave her a big hug and a kiss on the cheek,

"Can we talk about this more sometime?"

"*Definitely.*" I smiled. And with that, she stepped out and waved goodnight.

The next day I made plans to meet her for lunch. We ordered from the menu. She began fiddling with her hands, wrapping and unwrapping her napkin.

"You know, I had a relationship once," She looked away from me shyly, "with another woman."

"-Whaaaaaaaaat!" I grinned ear to ear and pointed my fork at her, "Spill it *sister!*"

Frida told me about her first long term relationship, which was with a woman, and how it had sadly ended around the same time she met her future ex-husband.

I leaned back in my chair and starred at the ceiling. "Wow. Ok! (I see that),"

I dug into the food I'd absentmindedly set aside. The lesbian life story of a dignified woman in her late seventies was worth every ounce of my attention.

"You know?" She whispered in a fragile tone, "I've never told anyone my story."

I stopped chewing and squeezed her hand. "I'm so glad you did." I shimmered.

She fell silent. I could tell her story held a measure of relief

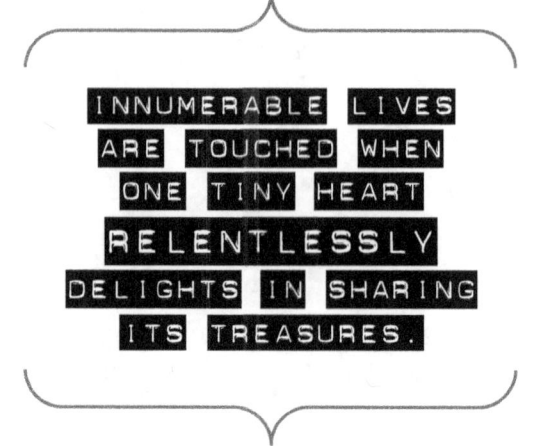

INNUMERABLE LIVES ARE TOUCHED WHEN ONE TINY HEART RELENTLESSLY DELIGHTS IN SHARING ITS TREASURES.

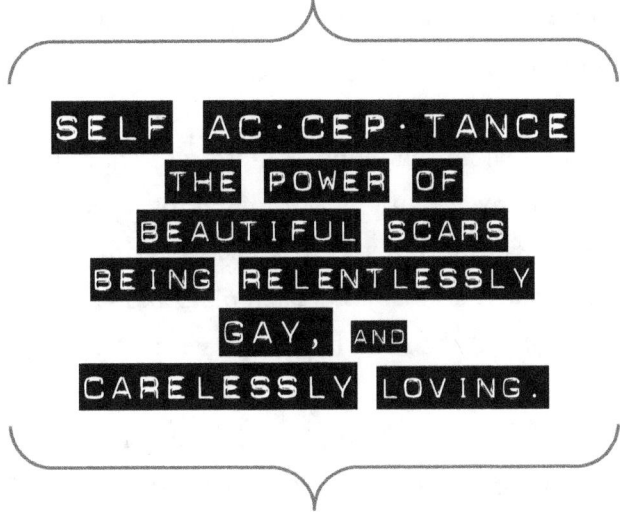

SELF AC·CEP·TANCE
THE POWER OF
BEAUTIFUL SCARS
BEING RELENTLESSLY
GAY, AND
CARELESSLY LOVING.

and pain. There is an immense vulnerability that comes with the deep relief of *being seen*, especially when that truth revolves around being *loved*. We sat there together smiling, hand in hand. *I was so proud of her.*

"Let's celebrate." I jested.

"How so?"

"-Let's drink!" I winked, knowing the two of us were epic fails at holding our liquor.

"Ohhhh no!" She giggled, batting me away with her napkin,

"That's the last thing I need!" she sat up straighter, smoothing the napkin back over her lap.

I stirred my iced tea, twirling my mustache like a bemused villain.

I got such a kick out of her.

She looked me straight in the eye with this delicious *aliveness* I hadn't seen before. I paused,

"I think I'm a lesbian." She said, soft as lightning.

"Okay! (I see that)," I agreed.

"You get to be *whatever* you want, Frida. You can be that with me."

The subject bounced around; We talked about her actual love interests. She considered looking up her old girlfriend, and her fears about telling her son and grandkids.

"My advice?" I said, "It's way too early to talk to them. You just stepped into a part of yourself you've been hiding a really long time. You don't need to worry about what anyone else has to say right now, Frida. This is a time for *you* to enjoy your Self. Get to know you. Take yourself on a date. Figure out what you like about *you* first. Then you won't worry about what to say to your family, you'll just know. Then you'll know it doesn't matter. And they'll hear you."

Frida took my advice and became a whole new person, enjoying her life wholly without the need to share it aloud. Rather than hiding that part of herself, she planted it in her heart. A seed of hope and mercy that she watered a little each day. She waited for it to naturally spill out into her life. People asked her what *happened* to make her so happy and she just smirked, "Life." Her new found spark also rekindled a loving relationship between her and her granddaughter, whom she'd unconsciously pushed away for wearing masculine clothes.

A few months passed and I noticed Frida had dropped off the radar. I called her up. "Good, I'm glad you called," she said, weirdly bashful. "I'm in Hawaii on vacation with my friend and her family. When I get back, we have to talk. There's something I need to tell you,"

"I don't like surprises," I warned. "You didn't go to Hawaii because you're dying, right?"

"It's not that bad!" She laughed heartily.

"Good! Then whatever it is, it doesn't matter," I assured her, "Let's meet."

I came over to her house for dinner a week later. I watched her set the food out on the table as we talked. "So what's the surprise?" I started bouncing in my seat.

"-just hold on!" She said as she tiptoed a full gravy bowl into its saucer and rounded the corner one more time. I watched her set a bowl of potatoes down and seat herself, winded. I often forgot how difficult menial tasks were to someone who was easily twice my age and kicked myself for not being a more gracious guest. "Thank you for inviting me over," I said humbly, "This looks beautiful."

We spooned out our portions, filling the silence with the *clanks* and *clinks* of each plate and glass. I watched her as I ate. She pretended not to notice. She agitated the salad bowl with white Alice in wonderland spoons.

"There's… There's this *man*," She began to stutter. She'd fallen for her best friend's son, a man in his late fifties she'd been acquainted with for the better half of ten years. She felt ashamed and ground her explanation to a halt. Her spoons loomed over the bowl of half masticated lettuce.

"It's okay!" I squinted through my smile.

"I can see that you like him!"

"What! I thought you'd be mad!"

"What? Why?"

"Because… he's a *man*!" She struck the air in protest.

Over the past 15 years, whenever she'd chased someone, she came up empty handed. This had happened so often, she gave up hope. Now, all of a sudden, she had this breakthrough in her identity and a whole new possibility of love showed up in her life.

But, as she explained, he was precisely the *opposite* of what she'd imagined.

"Why would I be mad?" I leaning in closer, "Do you know why this boy hadn't shown up in your life until *now*?" She shook her head. "Because darlin', you didn't have room for anyone else *until* you made room for yourself."

She nodded slowly.

Her mischievous spark spread from her eyes to her smile.

Every time Frida had looked down on herself, she stomped out a little bit of her spark. 15 years later, she sometimes wondered aloud *why was she alive at all?*.

HER LOVING SPARK LAY PRESSED BETWEEN SOGGY LAYERS OF SELF CONTEMPT.

Once Frida settled into herself and knew what *she* wanted, everything else became easy. As her Self appreciation overflowed her whole expression in life fundamentally changed. As she secretly let her heart off the hook for loving someone different, Frida *literally* embodied the gorgeous soul that everyone *already* saw in her!

This infinitely expanded her possibility's to include a boy's spontaneous invitation, later that year, to be abundantly loved for the rest of her life. She hadn't anticipated that her lover would come in *whatever* gendered package was lying around at the time, but she was wise enough not to waste her time feeling sorry or bad about it. She accepted the opportunity to love *herself* again and love just *showed up*. It's true. Sometimes we are not ready to love ourselves fully. How we delight in wasting our lives on the melodrama! Holding ourselves hostage to the end.

But let me ask you this:

When will we say, "I have had enough!"?

When can we say "I've paid my dues. I've earned the freedom to delight in my *own* self,"?

When will we resign as our own persecutor and ready-made victim?

It's when we replace our daily emotional crucifixion with generous, bright-eyed shamelessness that we can experience an abundance of companionship and emotional support; as we are then, first and always, our own best friend!

Honest self appreciation that offends all sense of modesty; that is what it takes to achieve greatness.

I'D RATHER BE VAIN THAN SELF DEFEATED.

Frida showed gratitude to her persona by embracing her Self *as is*. Even when she didn't know what that meant for her, she had faith in her Self (i.e. self love).

Now, If someone loves the very thing you hate, and the very thing you hate is *you*, aren't you the very enemy of all who love you? And if you hate your Self, aren't you the very best of friends with those who *hate* and *curse* you? You are, after all, in agreement to destroy *you* together. Furthermore, how can your beloved love you *without* your consent?

For Love without consensus (i.e. consent) ceases to resemble Love *at all*.

But by *being* the consummate lover of her own *persona,* Frita had not only protected her heart from self hatred/defeat, but also opened wide the possibility of someone else agreeing to *her* greatness and loving her back.

Self love is the *beginning* of all wisdom: the strongest form of forgiveness. For who can say they love someone of whom they continually demand *payback* (i.e. revenge)?

Love is the strongest form of forgiveness.

THE ART OF

OBJECTION

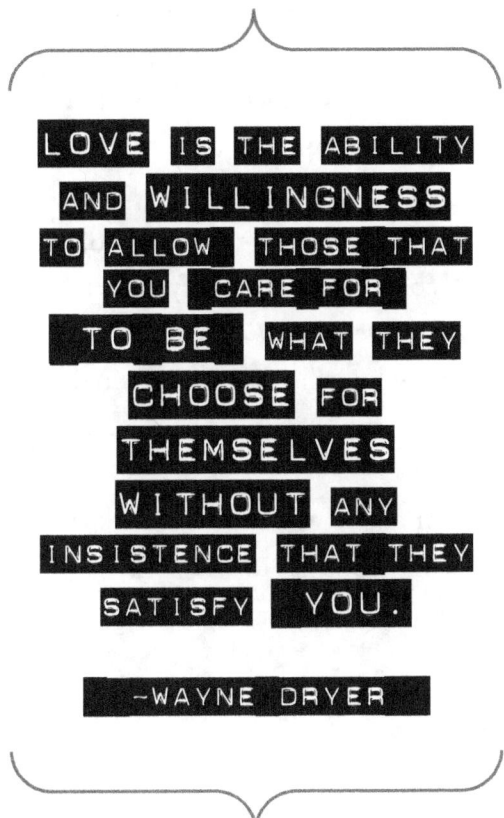

LOVE IS THE ABILITY AND WILLINGNESS TO ALLOW THOSE THAT YOU CARE FOR TO BE WHAT THEY CHOOSE FOR THEMSELVES WITHOUT ANY INSISTENCE THAT THEY SATISFY YOU.

-WAYNE DRYER

My father strummed his thick fingers heavily along the tabletop. He ran his hand over the edges like a carpenter assessing the work.

"I don't like what you're doing," he frowned. "You know I can't (emotionally) support the decisions you're making." He grimaced. I remember my father tactics: destroy combatants by approaching them as their superior. He was, after all, a U.S. marine first.

"I know." I said gently. "I'm okay with that."

"Just don't expect me to call you *he* at any time! You're my daughter, and you'll always be my daughter, and there's *nothing* you can do about that." He settled back into his chair with a triumphant glare.

His face read *naa na naa na naaaaaaa.*

His conversation was over. And that's where I stepped in, "I'm okay with that." I said reassuringly.

He didn't believe me, so I continued, "-but you know? At *some* point you might want to rethink that. I mean, you're gonna look a little crazy calling me *she* at a restaurant when my beards out to *here,*"

I struck out my chin and cupped an invisible cloud of proud, curly beard.

His jaw went slack as he stared, dumbstruck. *Chalk one up for the rebellious kid.* He hadn't thought of this logistical snafu. My response was not the rebellious emotional eruption he'd anticipated. I was clearly glad he was talking, okay with rejection, and my only objection was no less than a calm appeal to reason. I could hear his gears grinding for any answers to this strange new person he was seeing, perhaps, for the first time.

I felt a strange empathy and went to let him off the hook. After all, I was okay with being made *wrong*. It didn't change the facts: I'm no less a unicorn and I'm no less his kid.

And after making me *wrong* for the past 22 years, I wasn't even a nanometer less weird or off-putting in his eyes. I hooked my hands around his thick arm.

"Dad? I'm really okay with you *not* being okay with this. *It's okay.*"

I was sincere.

His features softened as his arm went around me. My dad, this big bumbling 'Homer Simpson' was still an irreplaceable part of my life. He messed up a lot of things in my rearing years, but when his hazardous moral iceberg melted, he was still a pretty lovable guy. He just needed permission to stick his flag in the moral high ground. He needed to be deemed *right* so we could all move on.

After all, I hadn't been financially or emotionally dependent on him since I was 15, so he had *nothing* to wager against my being precisely what I wanted, and we both knew it. The only thing he could have threatened to take away was himself, but we both knew he was too afraid to die a lonely asshole. Even if my dad had threatened to walk away, I had already said it was *okay*, so there would be no dramatic fanfare.

We still talk sometimes. Last time I saw him, he proudly introduced me as his *son*. I still wonder if it was not but for pride. It'd be a shame to admit your daughter's beard is coming in better than any of your other boys.

Now when he rants against my gender, I playfully remind him of this great little red button they install on these cell phones nowadays that quickly ends *unwanted* conversation. I clarify my boundaries with my father to honor my *own* heart in such a way that we can *both* laugh about it later. I'm really okay with him *not* being okay with what I do. I know he still wants to *want* to be okay. His struggle is not with *me*, it is with himself.

I have no intention of rescuing him from resolving his own problem.

I'm only compelled to object at being demoralized as a *person*. After all, *he* was the one who spawned this gender heretic. I had no choice in the matter. And, if there is any doubt as to where my optimistic *insanity* originated, I have a mirror on hand *just* for him. What better way to explain my disproportionate wellbeing than his inverted reflection?

IF YOU WISH TO KNOW COMPASSION, FIND WHERE YOUR ENEMIES WEEP.

—BRENNAN MANNING

Hi, I'm a happy transsexual.

Changing the idea of my identity through language has given me a most fantastic gift: the opportunity to author my own body and life. I know a slew of others who've done the same thing. One doesn't *need* a sex change to own one's identity, but it certainly makes this evolution much more visible.

We Agobi's are a symptom of a much greater evolution of consciousness. We are a people who rename *ourselves*, reconstruct and unfurl *our* identity in metamorphic stages, resculpt our own physical body, and singlehandedly override our role in society. We are unsuspecting geniuses, actively expanding the horizon on what it means to be *human*. Medical science may be catching up to our history of near *invisible* existing, but no one is talking about *what* our appearance foretells.

By seizing our spiritual heritage (through altering our bodies and controlling the course of our *own* lives), Transsexuals are about to bring civil rights *full circle*. For if a transman is now able to carry and bear his own children, and a transwoman is able to nurse until they are weaned, then what is there to stand in the way of women gaining access to freely choose body modification or reproductive sterilization from the age of consent *onward*?

The suffering I'm referring to is not from our inability to change our bodies, but in our being subjected to third party morality. This has justified our systematic genocide for the past millennia. Prejudice has divorced us from designing our own skin, which is our *birthright*.

There is nothing moral or natural about limiting our ordinary human ability to evolve beyond the boundary of punitive social constructs. By yielding to identity restrictions, we have not honored our Transsexual shamans and Agobi medicine women who have taught us:

Our bodies were made for our own delight.
And my body is none of your business.

I'm a happy Transsexual that suffers.

What is the source of my suffering?

It begins when my safety becomes threatened because I do not adhere to a *mythical* gender narrative simply because it is a *mass* delusion.

You have your own story about how to use your body and what it means to you. It has *nothing* to do with me. I believe in the path Transgender people make for themselves; where Princes kiss Frogs and Princesses slay dragons.

So while, the law fails to protect Trans from violence, we acknowledge we share in our fate *together*, even while we seem worlds apart. What befalls the Sheppard will soon happen to the sheep. The worlds of the 'is/isnts' and the 'go-betweens' (Agobi) are ever expanding into each other's lives.

It's my prayer that we end the suffering of those who are evolving into humane *humans*, so that together we may bring the world back into *balance*.

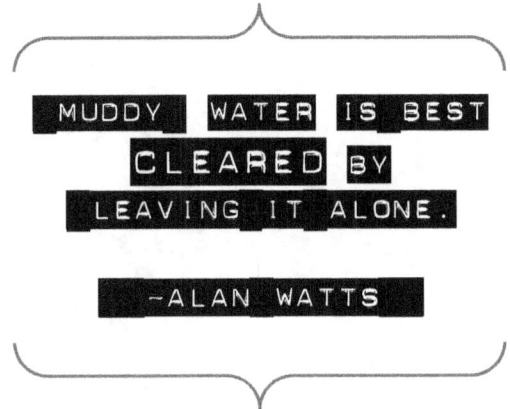

MUDDY WATER IS BEST CLEARED BY LEAVING IT ALONE.

—ALAN WATTS

I became an Agobi, that is, a spiritual midwife, when I acknowledged that my life functioned as such. Over and over, I continually appear to people at the crossroads of their identity and help them deliver some new aspect of themselves. And over and over, I'm presented with opportunities to spiritually midwife *change* through my conversations. This is what makes my being Transgender *perfect for the task*. As an Agobi, I have one hand in the world and one hand on the energy around me.

To fully walk in your identity, you must come to an agreement within yourself.

Who are you going to be?

To argue effectively with your Self, sometimes you need a spiritual midwife: someone to coach you through your labor towards a loved Self and, consequently, a more loving Self. When I midwife someone else's objections, I step out of their way and let them see *themselves*. This does *not* mean that I become their emotional punching bag *either*.

It's my job to momentarily suspend my own judgments and my need for validation so they can get to the root of *their* problem. It is, after all, an argument they're having with themselves. I must quiet my own objections long enough to make room for them to process theirs first. Objection is an important emotion we must allow others, especially when it impedes their progress to connect with us and move on.

If we continue creating hypersensitivity around gender identity, or exhibiting censorship within our own queer community, we will cut people off from making progress with us (without being offended by us) as we're too busy being offended *for them*. Policing and censoring someone's identity is damaging. No matter how offensive it is to us, we limit *our* own freedom to express ourselves when we *limit theirs*.

For example: I was recently asked to not use the word "Tranny" to describe myself, as it's an offensive term to some in the LGBT community. I agree that calling *anyone* names is inappropriate. I also have the right to refer to *myself* as anything I like. I refer to *myself* as a tranny affectionately and in memory of those friends who were killed for being *themselves*. I, like everyone else in the room, have an equal right to *own* my own identity, and express it in my *own words*, no matter who it offends. No one has the right to censor "I" but me.

Be free to describe yourself without permission. Be gentle with your words when describing others, as you will *never* know them as well as they do. They get to call their own identity, just as you do.

SEX CHANGES EVERYTHING

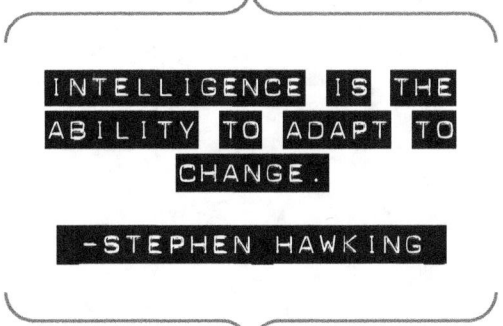

INTELLIGENCE IS THE ABILITY TO ADAPT TO CHANGE.

-STEPHEN HAWKING

I have a story about how sex changes everything, including conversation:

When I first took hormones, 5'5" was normal.

But now, 5'5" is too short.

Before, my hands were unnoticeable.

Now my hands are too small.

Before, my hair was beautiful and important to talk about.

Now having hair at all is seen as a good thing.

And before, people assumed I had a dress in my closet, whereas now they'd shame me if they found that dress in my closet today.

Everywhere I look, people narrate my sex with mythological stories. The timid female myths make people fight me when I'm bold and commanding. A multitude of stone tablets metaphorically rain down upon me from the mountain of man-made gods, commanding "what I should like" and "what I should wear" and "what I should be". Each inscribed with the heresy contradictions, one for a 'real' man, and one for a 'real' woman.

When my burden first took me on this spirit walk up the mountain into the realm of 'god men', I hadn't changed into a man. I was one who simply remained wild. I had always owned my own body and I let no one give chase, so I lacked the domestic yoke that would have kept me at home.

There at the top, I realized the truth about the male and female sex:

None of these motherfuckers have a clue what they're talking about! They look, but they can't see. They merely make a great noise, heaping heavy stones upon our backs to domesticate us with their burdens: Stones they have no strength to bear themselves. They give throw cheap tokens to women who cut themselves the deepest with rouge and hoes and extended heel.

There, I dropped the tablets from around my neck and climbed back down to be with my sisters. But they saw me bear the marks of male masters: a beard and a stature of my own. My sisters mistook me for a man, and although I turned the keys over to them, many won't walk out of the houses that were forged to entomb them; mistaking their depth for height.

In the end, I walked away empty handed. My gender remains mine to this day. I teach a new narrative now and I will grow my beard like a prayer to my sisters, until they all hear that same strength of voice inside of them as what booms incoherent from atop that man-made mountain.

We are all free, but some are not friends. They are addicted to making noise, flapping their jaws like ruminating cattle. Wagging their fingers at what they see out of place: at the world, and at us. Don't pay them any mind. They look, but they can't see in. As much as they state false like fact, they can't see past my skin or behind my eyes. So don't fret. You will always be invisible in their world.

But you will also always be free. Be delighted to be rid of them.

A straight man sat worlds across from me at the table. The cheerful yellow décor in this diner outlined his country profile. He wore a gleaming grin like a boy getting away with a dubious secret.

How appropriate I silently jested, returning the grin. I admit, he looked like he'd probably just escaped a wondering housewife at home.

Probably told her something like *he's got to go fix his friend's car again. Probably a "trans-mission'.*

Now, I don't pretend to know what he did with the rest of his life, and that's not why we were there. We were there to negotiate before we went to bed together. I could just see *desperate* under his skeptic exterior. I'm used to his type. He said in that "good 'ol boy" southern drawl,

 "So, yeeeu wawnt me tuh treat yeh like a *grrl?* er a *mayn?*",

[TRANSLATION] "So, you want me to treat you like a girl? Or a man?"

He chewed on his party toothpick.

"*Who*a! That came up fast…" I laughed tensely. The door swung open and a cold wind blasted me through and through. I shielded my eyes.

Life resembles the weather here, I thought wryly.

I hadn't expected that until the food got here, at least.

I set my hands on the table and laced my fingers back together. *You're losing points here, pal.*

These murky thoughts that put *my* gender on trial blasted me with another cold wall. I shuddered. I got that weary feeling of being hidden in plain sight and sighed. Hugging myself, I stared off. The linoleum lines became apparent all around me: yet another sign that his gendered world had begun to descend.

Black *or* white. Him *or* Her. Girl *or* Man.

My shoulders shivered as I gathered my thoughts.

I hate this color of yellow on the walls, I think, *Yeah. It's the color of smoker's teeth.*

Cowboy made a smug nasally noise over his coffee as I spotted an elderly couple sitting across the aisle from me. The old man was talking to his eggs while the woman's worried eyes met mine.

I know, me too. I thought.

Of course she looked worried. She was the only one *listening.* And who could blame her? What- with her husband who'd probably talked more to his eggs than to her face over the past 10 years? I would probably look worried too.

I didn't seem *right* to her. I knew this.

I smiled back appreciatively, but upon recognition, she turned away.

Strange how we act when we're finally acknowledged. I sighed again and drifted back to cowboy, now waiting for an answer. He tapped his toothpick on the table a few times before sticking the frayed end back in his mouth and twirling it around. The lines on his shirt looked dirty for some reason. I wondered how deep that went.

That's when I decided this date was pretty much over, so I digressed.

"Let me ask you what you mean by this and let's see if I understand." I said thoughtfully.

He nodded and folded his arms, pervishly enthusiastic.

"Are you asking me whether I should *not* look you in the face when you talk to me? Or, whether I should ridicule you when you cry?" His toothpick froze, stunned.

"No- What? Nah! That's not what I meant at all! I think you're rullll nice. Hot too. I just wanna know how'n I should treat you is all."

I smirked playfully, "Oh, I get it. I do." I consoled him. "Just hear me on what I'm saying."

I paused with a smile. "I think I know what you're *actually* asking. You want to know what to expect of me and how to react, right?"

He nodded slightly, a little more en garde and a little less confident. He braced his toothpick.

"I know when you look at me, you don't know whether to look *up* or *down*," I indicated at his chest and below his belt.

"Lets try- how about- let's just… *try* treating me human?"

"I awways do thaht!" He protested.

But he didn't; and worse yet, he didn't know it. I held my hand up to shush him and pressed,

"I don't think you know what I'm talking about here, so I'll say it another way. By 'girl or man' do you mean "should you eat me out front?" Or, "It's okay to just come at me from *behind*?""

He politely coughed aloud, trying to cover the bombshell I just laid out on the table.

I grinned widely. *I live for this.*

I kept my proposition playful as I continued: "Or are you asking: When you're mad, is it *more* appropriate to slap me and call me a bitch? Or should you just shout at me, for fear we end up kicking each other's ass?"

I paused. *He looked a bit frazzled* so I took his hand. His eyes flashed to the waitress just then, who set our breakfast plates down. He looked at his plate and quickly withdrew, folding his arms tightly against himself.

"I'm sorry… I- I cain't…" He said to his eggs.

Uh huh. I let him steep a little while I crammed my mouth full to mask my scowl.

"Do you phee what juspht happnnd theer?" I teased, spraying flecks of egg as I waved my fork around like a laser pointer at this gender game that good 'ol boy took as serious as a seizure.

I wasn't there to sleep with him anymore. This had just become a fascinating observation in the department of keeping white male privilege from falling before the *public's eye*.

He frowned. His brows furrowed as his toothpick drooped. Yep. He was angry I had made him *see* it, and reconsider his circumstance.

"I don't think that's fair." He murmured, "I wouldn't treat *you* that way! All I'm askin' is, like, how would you *like* to be treated? Like a woman, er a man?"

"Well," I asked, gently clearing my throat, "How would *you* like to be treated?"

"Like a man!" He smiled while he stuck his thumbs under each arm and puckered out his chest.

"What does that *mean*, exactly?" I asked.

"A man likes to open the door for you and get the checks and stuff like that."

He dropped the act and leaned in for the kill, "How would you like to be treated?"

His voice was seductive now. *Last chance*, his eyes read. Now it was my turn to frown.

"I wanna be treated like *Sean*." I finally relented, stirring my coffee cup with an agitated, *ting ting.*

"Well, what does *that* mean?" He bent his toothpick in half, and waved away the waitress from his coffee. I had to chew on that a moment. I heard so many questions in his inquiry; it was all so hard to separate. I squinted,

"The only way I can tell you is if I list the ways I *don't* like to be treated." I finally said.

I could tell he was getting tired of the game, but wanting the point, he took the bite.

"...fair 'nough. Like what?"

"Well, like I don't enjoy how people change the way they treat me based on how they perceive my gender and then later have the gall to say *I'm* the contradiction."

"Well, like what?"

I took a deep breath,

"Well. Like people who pretend they are advocates for my *personal* equality when they're really just interested in being *likeable* long enough to extort me. And like when people's expectations change of me."

"How?"

"Like I annoy people for talking too soft, when *before* I annoyed people for talking *at all*."

He thought about this a moment, silently agreeing.

"Like, depending on what people see my gender as, they either say I'd better grow my hair out *or* they wish I wouldn't keep it so long. They complain that I'm too flamboyant in public *or* complain that I can't cook worth a shit. People wrote me off as a fat girl *long before* they made fun of me for being a *short* guy."

The cowboy paused, genuinely intrigued. I began to feel those lines close up around me.

I continued, "I hate hearing this gender muck echo through the *same* lover! 'Oh. I wish you had breasts,' then, 'I wish you had bigger junk down there'! It's exhausting being told I have *too* much leg hair, then *not enough* facial hair. And what's worse? *Knowing* what they are wondering when they ask *what I am*. Like: Is it more appropriate for 'my type' to complain how much it costs to dress up my current female 'commodity', or more appropriate for me to feel *afraid* when you lean in to say,

"God, you look so pretty in those pants,"? Should I invite you to hang out on boy's night? Or should you *not* expect an invite because 'it's between us girls'?"

I let my confessions paint my world all around him, erasing the evidence of lines and boundaries that had kept him safe until now. By the unnerved look on his face, he'd assumed they'd always be there for him.

Welcome to my world, I nodded.

"Sure, everyone smiles and gives lip service to tolerance and gender variance, but it's the ugly truth that's comes out in overly *casual* conversation that makes me wonder if other people are capable of accepting differences that clearly transcend them. So when you asked me *how* I wanted to be treated... All I'd heard was, '*So. Which way do I discriminate?*'"

I finished talking and wondered at his sad eyes,

When I leave tonight, will you say I was half the man you were? Or tout that I was just some ugly bitch?

Well, he sat there a quick minute and stared back. His toothpick was demolished. I saw a boy who'd once forgotten the difference between the question and the lie.

"So? *What are you?*" he asked again hesitantly, trying to put some distance between himself and me at the table.

"I'm Sean." I said, "What are *you?*" I invited him in again, *Please. Do surprise me,* I begged.

"I'm a straight man." He mimicked, I'm sure for the millionth time.

"Oh? Ooooh..." My smile faded. "Oh, I... I'm sorry-... " I feigned embarrassment as I got up from the table to leave.

"What? What! What is it? What's wrong?!" Stunned, his hands grasped the tables edges, confused. I grabbed my coat from the bench and turned to face him.

"It's just- It's just... you know? I don't date straight men..."

I zipped up my coat, and took a step back. "You got the check, *right?*" I turned from his smoldering look, stepped around the waitress, and struck my foot against the door to barrel it open,

"*Bitch-*" He seethed.

I stopped dead, halfway in the icy doorframe and turned to face the confused looking waitress who seemed to have been caught between us. I gave her a saucy heathen grin,

"It's okay, honey! He just says that because *I have a vagina.*"

I spewed loudly to the thousand silent screaming faces in the dining hall, including his own.

I never seen a man shrink to the size of a knarled up stump like that.

I gleamed with every ounce of pussy pride I could muster and stared straight into that waitresses eyes as the jaws dropped around me. I heard a distant toothpick hit the floor in the silent restaurant as I slipped the waitress five bucks,

"Hey. Do me a favor?" I hid my mouth with one hand, and loudly pointed at the stump with my other, "He wants to be treated like a *mayn...* See that you do that for him, *wouldja?*"

I winked at her slightly bemused face and turned back out the door to step into the world of grey.

Before our conversation at that restaurant, I'd wondered if we *had* dated*, would he have complained that I am too expressive in public or because I can't cook worth a shit?*

Now I had my answer.

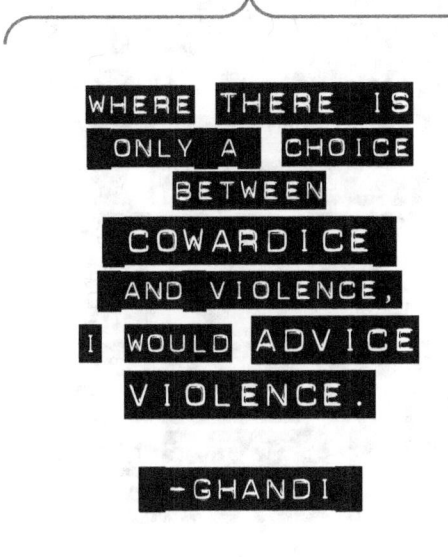

WHERE THERE IS ONLY A CHOICE BETWEEN COWARDICE AND VIOLENCE, I WOULD ADVICE VIOLENCE.

-GHANDI

Language does not indicate whether something is real or not. Words are only *sometimes* referring to actual tangible things. Identity interests me because it's paradoxically a thing that *isn't*: a projection of an unmanifested object. Language is merely *meaningful* rather than something that manifests. Hence, there's no point in arguing with someone about the correctness of your identity, as they cannot make *anything* of you appear or disappear by merely stating so. Whether I think my "I" is masterful or obscene, either way *I am correct*. It's *my* insight about "I" that holds lasting consequences.

Adding morality, the *rightness* or *wrongness* of a thing, into the concept of identity is like mixing salt with your drinking water. Sure, you may feel satisfied for the moment, but too much will drive you *mad*. Staunch moralists are unable to function without laying waste to their community because the obsession with *rightness* makes one intolerant to both change and possibility. Adding morality to the conversation of identity is like painting over the windshield and looking to the rearview mirror for direction. Sure you'll go places; you'll just have to plow people down in your wake.

Another thing I've observed is that all things meaningful come with *names*. We gives names to add meaning to an object or a concept. We even refer to it as 'name calling' when one abuses that meaning. So, if someone picks a moral fight with you over the *wrongness* of your identity, listen to their language. By acting like they *know* you, they then speak to you as their *inferior* with names like: "sinner", "loser", etc. This projects a false image of *unworthiness* and *guilt*. By stating to you who you are and what *your* problem is rather than asking and listening, moralists seek to hijack one's identity in order to reinforce their delusion of *self importance*. This is why a moralist cannot stand when he is not *heard*, as his whole existence revolves around creating stumbling blocks for others.

When you participate in the madness that is the argument of *moral rightness*, you only feed the monster. Do as I do: Politely (and loudly) disrupt each statement with *out-loud* disbelief, "No, that's *not* really me," or *tsk tsk* their presumption of you *while* not consoling them, or their accusations. In the end, a moralist can only appear more ignorant after dramatizing about whom they *really never knew at all*. And rightly so. Any argument over the rightness or trueness of one's identity is doomed to go adrift. Don't take responsibility for their confusion; they were floundering to take a stab at someone long before you arrived.

Personally, I let them drown in the madness. Or, by participating in the conversation for entertainment, I can play alongside a heated moralist while purposefully misdirecting their aim. You may not only *enjoy* the game they are playing, ('I have more value/answers than you do'), but they will also be at an utter loss to define the "*real*" you that keeps slapping their verbal hand away. Some savvy moralists may even point this out, by which I always agree with them!

MORALIST: (repeats) "You are a _____."
ME: "As you can *see*, I am clearly *me*."
MORALIST: "If you are not a _____, then what *are* you?"
ME: (grinning) "Freed from the tyranny of your accusations, sir!"

If you become good at this preoccupation with playing on the moral high ground, you can dance around who you truly are without raising bristles. Either way, the company

ADDING MORALITY TO THE CONVERSATION OF IDENTITY IS LIKE PAINTING OVER THE WINDSHIELD AND LOOKING TO THE REAR VIEW MIRROR FOR DIRECTION. SURE YOU'LL GO PLACES; YOU'LL JUST HAVE TO PLOW PEOPLE DOWN IN YOUR WAKE.

you keep will always only be able to *assume* who they think you are. If they're intelligent, they'll recognize this. Describing you as *unknowable* would be the closest to understanding the truth of human identity.

Ultimately, it's kinder to happily walk away from a moralist. They may come unglued at your identity's paradox of contradictions. But you cannot satisfy their thirst, *so don't try.*

THEY HAVE THE MADNESS.

And their argument is not worth defending.

Identity is thus: If it remains unspoken, it is unknowable, irreproachable, intangible, malleable, and inarguable.

Without a word to state, a person may indeed become *all* things to *all* people.

Moralists are vain creatures, only existing by their continually talking about themselves. More importantly, moralists are neither good nor evil and, if you disappear from conversation (*i.e. you listen*), you can clearly observe the person opposite you. So long as you've internalized the concept of being your own version of *Self*, there is no harm in befriending a staunch moralist. For whom can say that your art is *wrong*?

Furthermore, if my boss happens to be a sex/gender moralist, why would I allow him to bring my gender up in conversation? I could maintain a peaceful and friendly low-key acquaintance with a sexist boss while avoiding idle chat. I can't be a target if I don't *exist* to him, so I remain invisible by refusing to engage in any salty topics of conversation. Were he to inquire of my sex or gender or sexuality *directly*, I would detour his moral assessment and leave his inquiry feeling ridiculous, unwelcomed, and unprofessional.

Why misdirect someone in knowing the *actual* me? Several reasons. People use age old stereotypes to suffocate another's magical well being. Why? Because authentic identity is subversive and can't be controlled (because it doesn't have a name). For example: If someone keeps absentmindedly ridiculing me by calling me a faggot, I'll still speak to them in a respectful manner. Eventually, they may realize their comment only makes them look more and more like a useless asshole. I do (internally) acknowledge when something like that is *hurtful*. But instead of being mean to that person, I ask myself "*Where* does it hurt?"

Truth is, I don't know where it hurts (it's intangible), but I have to admit: It has nothing to actually do with *that* person. Something inside *me* is reacting to it, with or without them there to point it out. So when I emotionally hurt, I deal with *me*.

However, if someone calls me a faggot with the sole intention to hurt me, I remove myself from the conversation all together. Words are wasted on people who beg for power.

As my grandpa used to say: *you can't fix stupid.*

A person who is wise realizes they don't know you well enough to say who you are. And a true friend will never assume they have the right to define your identity *for* you.

The fact is: If I remain silent in conversation, I simply cease to exist. Being a person without identity is a *really* powerful way to navigate a conversation.

That's what we mean when we say '*anonymous*', is it not?

Therefore, if I wish to remain *visible* to someone, I must express what my "I" means to me, with or without words. That is entirely what we do on a blind date: Chat the whole night in order to *appear to them through language.*

When people verbally attack "I", they are actually *only* attacking a story I have created *about* me, which is *not* actually me, but merely a projection of what 'I' *means* to me.

When a person attacks me on a personal level, they can only either:

1. Use an erroneous observation *they* have made about me.
2. Use an erroneous observation *someone else* has made about me, or
3. Use an observation *I've* voiced about myself (i.e. *my* narration of my own identity) *against* me.

None of which is actually real, personal, or of any value to me *without my consent.*

In other words, why would I waste my time on their *self infatuated* objections?

If I visually and verbally create an image of identity that I love and affirm, any other negative projection they make appears as the weaker argument from an addle headed nobody.

I exist *purely* in my description of me, therefore, if I describe myself to others as a confident person who possesses the qualities I see within myself, I generate interest in those around me who *need those qualities* in their life!

And when they called upon those attributes in me, I become what I describe.

PORTRAIT OF A

QWEIRDO

MAY YOU BE
UNHINGED
BY THE IMPLICATION
OF YOUR IDENTITY
AS

THE FICTIONAL NARRATION

OF SELF

THROUGH
MEANINGFUL STORIES.

S.G. MUNE

The most important thing in life is to be yourself.

UNLESS YOU CAN BE BATMAN. ALWAYS BE BATMAN.

AKA MOONY: TRANSGENDER EDUCATOR, TRAVELING GYPSY, AND AGOBI SPIRIT HEALER.

S.G. Mune ("Moon") first discovered how to write and draw to convey a message at 2 years old. These later became legible around 5 or 6... ish. 26 years later, S.G. utilized their talents to complete their first book, *The Myth of Gender,* on their return from psych. Along with being a motivational speaker on the power of Identity, they also enjoy comedy writing, educating on genderless rights, and life as a traveling gypsy. They currently live in Northwest North America with their dogs, Reese and Sydney. When S.G. is not traveling, they pound on their computer keyboard in the hope that they can create another portal through which to solve their life's riddle:

What is identity made of?

S.G.'s dream is to one day write from their own 'traveling home', as their spirit guides have promised.

GENDER ATHEIST BOOKS

LOOK FOR THESE OTHER WORKS!

THE MYTH OF GENDER 2

The second you pick it up, this book casts your Identity further down the rabbit hole than you *ever* before imagined! Covering new more controversial concepts, S.G. opens up on deeper topics such as: Quantum identity, The Spiritual Trans Identity, and the 6 Distinct Illusions of Self!

A FISTFUL OF PETALS

What kind of life leads to an Agobi Identity?
In his autobiography, S.G. Mune shares his inner thoughts over his many hilarious and tear jerking moments as a poly pansexual transgender gypsy, ex-mormon, ex-ordained minister, ex-female, and ex-ex-gay.

THE MYTH OF WAGE EQUALITY

Sean is currently looking to fund this independent study.
This project is poised to reach 6,000+ post hormone transitioned (HRT) Transmen across the United States, comparing their salaries pre and post hormones. The purpose of this study is to raise awareness of discrimination against women and transmen through wage based disparity by producing *actual numbers on wage changes* based on a person's perceived gender.
Please Contact the author if you wish to contribute to this project.

CONTACT ME

JOIN M.O.G. ON FACEBOOK:

www.facebook.com/MythofGender

OR SETUP
A LIVE SESSION ON GENDER IDENTITY
WITH

S.G. MUNE

VIA SKYPE, PHONE, OR CLASSROOM,

EMAIL:

GenderAtheist@gmail.com

SCRATCH PAPER

THOUGHTS, QUESTIONS, IDEAS, AND CHALLENGES

www.ingramcontent.com/pod-product-compliance
Lightning Source LLC
Chambersburg PA
CBHW080417290526
45791CB00008BA/2317